KEY CONCEPTS IN LITERARY THEORY

Key Concepts in Literary Theory

Second Edition

Julian Wolfreys, Ruth Robbins and Kenneth Womack

Edinburgh University Press

© Julian Wolfreys, Ruth Robbins and Kenneth Womack, 2002, 2006

Edinburgh University Press Ltd
22 George Square, Edinburgh

Typeset in Sabon
by Hewer Text UK Ltd, Edinburgh, and
printed and bound in Great Britain by CPI Antony Rowe, Eastbourne

First edition published in 2002 by Edinburgh University Press

Transferred to digital print, 2007

A CIP record for this book is
available from the British Library

ISBN 0 7486 2458 9 (paperback)

Contents

Preface to Second Edition

The second, revised edition of *Key Concepts in Literary Theory* has been expanded in two of its three sections, 'Concepts and Terms', and 'Chronology of Critical Thinkers, with Bibliographies'. With the intention of providing a more comprehensive coverage, and so filling in what, in retrospect, now appear obvious omissions, more than eighty terms and their definitions have been added to the first part of the volume. It is hoped that the changes provide additional usefulness to the reader, while, equally, the volume has retained the accessibility, ease of reference, and 'portability' of the first volume. Of the inclusions, the majority are drawn from psychoanalysis, reflecting the continued and sustained interest in this particular approach to literary studies, even while the fortunes of other discourses appear to have waned somewhat. Of the remaining other inclusions, several are 'formalist' in nature, concerned with grammatical, linguistic, and rhetorical terminology that has found a renewed currency in particular areas of discursively focused literary theory. Finally, with regard to inclusion, those concepts or terms not covered obviously by a psychoanalytic or linguistic rubric are drawn from historically or sociologically inflected or influenced critical modes. In the third part, the chronology, around forty additional critics, philosophers, and historians have been added. To the existing entries, a couple of major publications have been included, which appeared subsequent to the original publication of *Key Concepts* in 2002. As with the first edition of *Key Concepts*, in most cases and whenever possible, I have sought to give in-print paperback editions of as many of the publications as possible. The other changes made to the chronology are, sadly, death dates for several of the thinkers listed there.

As ever, once more, and no less sincerely, I would like to thank Jackie Jones at Edinburgh University Press. I would also like to take the opportunity to thank Ruth Robbins and Ken Womack for their work on the first edition. Any errors or infelicities, Austinian or otherwise, in the current edition are entirely my own.

Julian Wolfreys, London and Los Angeles July 2005

Foreword

Key Concepts in Literary Theory addresses the evolving nature of critical thinking within literary studies, particularly during the closing decades of the twentieth century – an era that saw a dramatic and highly diverse reconceptualisation of the theoretical project. During this period, literary studies reimagined itself along a number of philosophical, political and cultural axes. The questions asked of the literary text, questions which are still in the process of being articulated and reoriented, brought to bear upon the text interests and concerns from a number of disciplines, discourses and areas of study. In addition to canon expansion and redrawing the boundaries of critical theory regarding a variety of sociological fronts, scholars refined a host of new terms and concepts for examining the minute particulars inherent in gender studies, queer theory, poststructuralism, postmodernism, historical studies and cultural criticism, among a host of other theoretical worlds.

Key Concepts in Literary Theory is then a reference work which arises as a response to the transitions in literary studies. As such, it provides readers with an array of traditional and essential literary concepts and period terms – including *irony, existentialism, symbolism* and *modernism* – while also enumerating a wide variety of concepts associated with the advent of 'high theory' and the emergence of poststructuralist and postmodernist thought. From *aporia* and *liminality* to *phallocentrism* and *simulacra*, critical theory's increasingly hybrid and endlessly fecundating terminology confronts novice and advanced scholars alike with a host of linguistic and intellectual challenges. How, for example, does one situate his or her own notions of contemporary literary theory within the textual practices of a widely dispersed and vastly changing discipline? How, moreover, do students troll the often complicated shoals of literary scholarship and decode what they perceive and often resist as its specialised jargon and web of competing terms? How do students intervene in increasingly hybrid discourses so as to gain critical purchase and agency? Conventional dictionaries hardly begin to explain or account for the theoretical project's fluctuating and often chameleon-like lexicon. As a student recently put it to one of the authors of this glossary in response to an assigned reading on a 'theory' course, 'I looked up every word I didn't know in the dictionary and none of them were there!' It is even the case that traditional rhetorical terms or concepts drawn from other disciplines undergo the effects of tropological torque, so that, arguably, knowledge of the 'original' meaning, so called, is of limited use to the student reader.

Of course, in proposing a volume such as this and, moreover, a volume such as this which aims at once to be comprehensive *and* relatively small, we are leaving ourselves hostage to fortune, if not to reviewers. How do we justify inclusions or exclusions? One always wants to ask, especially of the more recent terms, why this and not this? How is the length of a definition to be determined? Which critical vocabularies are to be valued over others? Such questions, while valid, are unanswerable and no short reference work can truly be authoritative and inclusive; yet it seems, more than ever, a small, manageable reference work pertaining to what is called 'literary' or 'critical theory' is needed. Thus it is our intention to provide a succinct and reliable map to the terrain of critical discourse. In doing this, we are seeking not to provide a route map so much as to identify landmarks in an all too frequently difficult terrain. Of course, we run the risk of perhaps intimidating the occasional reader as much as seeking to help them. With this in mind, this volume should be seen as being conceived as much for discussion as it is for definition. This book is intended as a classroom aid, and with that in mind many entries will require further clarification, comment, discussion or elucidation, often with reference to further research, on the part of the professor. It is this work which *Key Concepts in Literary Theory* seeks to open, and to provide the means for inquiry, exploration and engagement.

While not being able to provide definitions for every possible term in the constellation of theoretically oriented discourse, this volume seeks to afford readers with a guide to critical theory's multifarious, rapidly shifting vocabulary, especially as a response and a responsibility to the student whose dictionary remains silent. In addition to devoting attention to the significant historical nuances of Russian formalism, reader-response theory and psychoanalytic criticism, the concepts explored in this glossary hint at the shape of literary theory's intellectual future. From *technoscience* and *cyberwar*, to *mnemotechnic* and *digitality*, the parlance of contemporary critical theory continues to develop concomitantly with the rhythms and moods of mass culture and technology. What is called, with ever greater potential vagueness, 'literary theory' has enjoyed a similar relationship with gender studies' larger connections with media and popular culture. Drawing upon such terms as *gender parody, cyborg, masquerade* and *avant-garde*, gender studies – as with other theoretical communities – continues to seek language forms that most precisely express, however strategically or provisionally, various aspects and manifestations of gender in contemporary life. By examining the recent emergence of theoretical terminology in concert with similar developments in contemporary science, technology, literature and culture, *Key Concepts in Literary Theory* underscores critical thinking's remarkable capacity not only for providing critique of literary texts, but also their synergy with the apparently *non*-theoretical issues that mark our lives (which is to suggest nothing other than the fact that these are the issues which resolutely reify or otherwise maintain an invisibility of the theoretical, epistemological and ideological interests which underpin the very idea that we live and think without 'theory', that is to say without forms of reflective, analytical or interpretative processes).

With regard to the choices which determine the content of the present volume, it is, we know, a source of profound irritation when writers and critics insistently refuse to write in words that we understand easily, especially when that comprehension is challenged concerning something apparently so much 'ours' as literature. Transparency is thought of as a great virtue; keeping it simple is propounded as an ideal. To describe someone's language as laden with jargon is a real insult, as is the suggestion that a scholar wraps up an otherwise straightforward point in a 'needlessly' dense, 'over-intellectualised' discourse (which process has also been described to us as 'pretentious'). But these are views which imply that difficult concepts should be laid out on a plate – anything that's too hard shouldn't be thought at all. That which is difficult is therefore immediately translated, without the reader being aware of the translation process as being in his or her hands, and being not so much a translation as it is an act of resistance – calling a halt to reading – in response to the allergen that is critical discourse. The student is, of course, not to blame for this: he or she is simply exhibiting the symptoms of reading propagated often outside, but also, dangerously, inside the university: a kind of journalistic facility determined institutionally as necessary to the pragmatics of learning which assumes the right to determine the velocity of reading, along with the fallacious assumption of a relationship between the visibility of the text and the transparency of the writing which composes the text. Visibility of meaning (that which, of course, is never simply *there*) somehow must assume a specific oscillation within the written word (which, of course, is resolutely *there* but which somehow is determined as acting as though it weren't) which, as a result, begins to vanish, to reveal what is being said, or should have been said, all along.

Literary and cultural theories problematise the tricky negotiation between visibility and transparency, and are particularly prone to coining new words – coining itself, of course, being a word that has to do with forgery, fakery, inauthenticity and the obfuscation of true value. But we suggest that you imagine for a moment a world in which there are no neologisms – no new words at all. Imagine our vocabularies frozen at a given point in history, with stringent laws that say there must be no more words. What point in history would be ideal, I wonder? The language of Shakespeare, maybe, except that would mean that we would have no vocabulary to cover modern technologies like cars, microwave ovens, speedy printing. Imagine the scenario where a student – not you but someone you know – is heard to say that the language of theory is unnecessarily difficult; then imagine, as part of this hypothetical scene, the same student remarking that the language of Shakespeare (or the eighteenth-century novel) is too difficult. Are we to do away with both 'languages'? Are the difficulties of the same order? And, if not, should we consider the difficulty not in the text but in the apprehension? And if we don't have the words, would we have the concepts, or the objects? Would it be possible to imagine new inventions, new ideas of any kind?

You will not, of course, be the first people to imagine such a world. George Orwell's 1949 dystopian vision of the future (ironically now in the past), *Nineteen Eighty-Four*, is an extended meditation on language frozen, on thought congealed. A particularly chilling moment is Winston Smith's conversation with a Newspeak dictionary maker named Syme who describes a sadistic pleasure in destroying language. 'Don't you see,' he says to Winston, 'that the whole aim of Newspeak is to narrow the range of thought? Every year fewer and fewer words, and the range of consciousness always a little smaller . . . there will *be* no thought, as we understand it now. Orthodoxy means not thinking – not needing to think. Orthodoxy is unconsciousness.' Winston looks in horror at Syme, realising not only the horrible nature of his project, but also that Syme himself, who 'sees too clearly and speaks too plainly' is ironically doomed despite his enthusiasm for Big Brother's project. Anyone who thinks like Syme will not survive in the world of *Nineteen Eighty-Four*.

But Orwell's novel makes the reverse point as well. If we have lots of new words, we are able to think lots of new thoughts. Unorthodoxy is consciousness, and consciousness takes place in a rich sea of words. We need the new words if critical thinking is not simply to become a repeated gesture, where students and teachers endlessly recycle the same old ideas about the same old texts. I don't want to be part of a project which merely rewards those who repeat what has been said before. Traditionalists are always talking about the 'dumbing-down' of culture; but there are few dumber things than a person who refuses to speak or write because the language is too difficult and too new.

This collection of words is not the last word: there will be other words you need to learn, and you will want to deepen your understanding of some of the terms that are only briefly glossed here. But this collection of words aims to get you to think new thoughts – thoughts you cannot have without the vocabulary in which to express them. Of course, slavishly using the words without thinking about them would simply make a new unconscious orthodoxy. But using the words creatively, pushing them to their limits: there is something to be said – and it is not a dumb something – in favour of that.

A number of the terms included in *Key Concepts in Literary Theory* are being defined in this kind of reference work for the first time. One of the reasons perhaps for their previous omission from otherwise exemplary reference books is that, beyond or before any question of neologism or novelty, there is a real issue of the problematic of definition and, concomitantly, indefinability. Certain keywords or terms indicate what might best be defined as quasi-concepts, terms which cannot properly be defined in any positive fashion. In order to be true, for example, to the term 'deconstruction' and its appearance in the work of Jacques Derrida, one can say what it is not, how it does not operate, and so forth; yet one cannot say with any fidelity what it is or might be, and this is for the reason that what Derrida might term the ontological question, that is to say the question of definition based on the idea that there is a determinable or determinate identity for 'deconstruction', cannot be given because there is no identity as such, even though many critics have misunderstood Derrida's use of the word. In another example, postmodernism is notoriously difficult to define because there is little agreement about the definition of this slippery term.

An aspect of pushing words to their limits is that the very grounds on which meaning is assumed become, if not untenable, then, at the very least, precarious. This does not mean that critics employ words in any way they like, or that they empty words of meaning. Indeed, quite the opposite is often the case. If a word, after having resided invisibly in the pages of a few dictionaries for a number of years, or, on occasion, centuries, suddenly or gradually comes back into focus, it chances to do so because of what haunts its etymological and semantic structures, what disjoints it anachronistically from within, if we can put it like that. A word, term or concept, trope or other figural manifestation returns precisely because in its etymology there remain various oscillations which, on the one hand, intimate an afterlife for the word, while, on the other, point up that something strange, something uncanny has always taken place within the structure of the word. Take a long forgotten term such as *deconstruction*, a supposedly familiar, supposedly accessible word such as *supplement*, or a term devoted to a specific discourse or scientific practice such as *anastomosis* – all are read and deployed in the field of criticism for the very reason that, within their structures, their histories or genealogies, there takes place even, or perhaps especially, at what we might provisionally call their 'origins' (and we can no longer assign such a notion unequivocally because this concept too has been complicated within the recent history of critical thinking) what might be termed an originary supplement: a doubting and/or division in the etymology of the word which, in displacing unequivocal meaning at the root, so to speak, disturbs the very idea of a discernible 'true' or unified starting point. Thus, it has been shown that there is not a single, simple origin or genesis *by the very multiplicity or excess of contradictory, if not paradoxical meanings or values inscribed in the structure of a word, and the radical undecideability which this puts to work.* (See the entry on *undecideability*.)

Thus it is not the case that critics are merely being modish in transforming words. Indeed, it is a case that, strictly speaking, the critic cannot be said to have transformed anything at all, other than (hopefully) the reader's comprehension by bringing into focus that which was there all along, albeit occluded, encrypted or repressed as the effect of either neglect or long familiarity. ('Accessibility' is the name we give to the language we have learnt so well that we have forgotten that we have had, at some time, to learn how to use it appropriately, in the proper contexts, and so on.) The transformation of words, as we imply above, is always already underway within particular terms and the critic, as the good reader (see *reader/reading*), has read what is taking place and not imposed something in the name of obscurity or pretension on an otherwise commonplace word.

Thus, it may be said, critical thinking involves itself, in some areas, with acts of 'remembering': remembering what has been archived, remembering what has been buried, remembering what is in plain view but at the same time erased, worn away, through centuries of linguistic usury – for if so-called new words are 'coined', to recall an earlier term, it follows that, in use, their textures, their complexities, their details, can, in the frequency of exchange (and words *are* a commodity, like or, at least, quite like any other), be worn out, partially effaced, until only the most vestigial and ghostly traces remain, as the remains of linguistic, semantic and etymological complexity. Thus, if you recall the argument presented above concerning that imagined, yet unimaginable scenario where language might become frozen at certain prescribed levels of undemanding accessibility and appropriate facility, such an impossible condition would exist, *could* exist, only through an exorcism of all the ghosts of language. If, as German philosopher Martin Heidegger asserted, language *is* the house of being (see *being*), then it is a house which is inescapably haunted, and it is precisely the condition of haunting for which we are, as readers, responsible, to which we have to respond, and with which we have to deal, without seeking to exorcise that which takes place as the possible condition of all communication and interpretation.

Perhaps what this means is that we have to learn to live with ghosts. Negotiating meanings of terms suggests an activity of mediating between what is visible and invisible in any linguistic and semantic structure, while acknowledging that there will often be that which remains just beyond our grasp. The development of conceptual terminology in the study of literature might be said to operate in the space between the visible and invisible. Seeking to define terms without entombing them, turning them into a corpse language, is a risky business, but it is to be hoped that what takes place here, for the reader of *Key Concepts in Literary Theory*, is an effort to attend to the spirit of language, rather than its letter.

The glossary of critical concepts and terms is accompanied by two other reference sections. With regard to cross-references, recognising that no term operates in isolation but is part of a network from which meaning emerges, we have highlighted those concepts, words and terms which occur on several occasions and which are defined herein. The first of the two reference sections of the present volume extends the principle of the glossary to provide brief definitions of various areas, movements and disciplines within critical study, each of which is accompanied by a bibliography of suggested reading. Each bibliography brings together 'introductory' texts, collections of essays, key volumes. Of course, each bibliography is necessarily selective, given the space here, and excludes far more than it can include. Following this is a chronology of thinkers from different fields, from Karl Marx to Judith Butler and Avital Ronell, to each of whom is appended a brief bibliography of recommended, essential reading. One reason at least for the inclusion of the second and third sections is to offer students an at-a-glance sense of the broad outlines of literary theory and to provide selective bibliographies of important works by critical thinkers whose names often appear most frequently in classes on the practice and theory of literary criticism. While we realise that the bibliographies appended here can always be quibbled over, we have generally sought to choose works that are both representative and available. The relation between the three sections of this volume is perhaps implicit rather than initially explicit, nonetheless a certain provisional contextualisation is offered while it has to be admitted that no context is ever finite or exhaustible. The chronology of critical thinkers is offered because definitions of keywords are offered throughout with reference to specific critics and philosophers and thus it is our hope that the student reader will pull together various strands throughout.

Concepts and Terms

A

Abject/Abjection—Term used by Julia Kristeva as an attempt to undo the **binary** logic of much psychoanalytic thought, where the concepts of (desiring) **subject** and object (of **desire**) often represent a co-dependent opposition. In order to understand Kristeva's point it is necessary that we recognise 'subject' and 'object' not only as opposed positions or two halves of a logical model, but also as supposedly discrete and complete identities in and of themselves. Each term is accorded its own self-sufficient meaning with definable boundaries. Such boundaries are the psychic limits by which the self separates itself from its other within the psychoanalytic framework of Kristeva's text. Another way of positing the subject/object dyad would be to comprehend it in terms of 'self/other'. The abject, says Kristeva, is 'neither subject nor object'; instead it opposes the ego by 'draw[ing] me to the place where meaning collapses'. While the subject/object structure makes logical meaning possible, but the abject is an **uncanny** effect of horror, threatening the logical certainty of either the subject/object or self/not-self binary. Abjection is thus the psychic experience of a slippage across the boundaries of the self, and with that a partial erasure of the borders of the psyche which define the ego. Absolutely essential to all cultures, the abject is, amongst other things, the fluid locus of forbidden desires and ideas whose radical exclusion is the basis of cultural development.

Absence/presence—Example of **binary opposition**, whereby, according to structuralist linguistics and, subsequently, structuralist critical analysis, neither term nor, in fact, the concept articulated by such a term generates its meaning without implicit acknowledgement of its opposite term and the necessary implication of one in the other. Jacques Lacan draws on the linguistic work of Roman Jakobson to explore the dynamic of absence/presence in the **symbolic** order. Jacques Derrida explores the interanimating relationship between the two terms in relation to the privilege in Western thought given to voice as guarantor of presence over the absence and implications of death signalled in any act of **writing**. When Derrida remarks that '*différance* is recognised as the obliterated origin of absence and presence' he demonstrates how binarisms are not composed of discrete, separable identities but are only capable of articulation through their invisible, fundamental interconnectedness.

Abstraction—Applied to the fine arts, the term refers to the abandonment of representational practices, with a concomitant emphasis on the part of artists on form and colour for their own sake.

Absurdism—French novelist and philosopher Albert Camus first suggested a philosophy of the absurd, and subsequently his work has come to be regarded as an absurdist expression concerning matters of politics and ethics. The term was taken up specifically with regard to theatre, and the phrase 'theatre of the absurd' is widely used in criticism. In Europe, chief practitioners of this perceived form of theatre were Ionesco, Fo and Beckett. Occasionally Harold Pinter has been included under such a rubric. Conventionally, theatre of the absurd involves presentation of the futility of human action or behaviour, and the anguish this causes in a meaningless world, rational explanation being unequal to providing purpose.

Actant—The term is used in the semiotic work of A. J. Greimas, referring to fundamental actions and character types. According to Greimas, actants exist at the level of action; characters function as actants when they question the nature of subjectivity.

Aesthetic/aesthetic theory—From Greek *aistetikos*, meaning perceptible to the senses, aesthetic approaches to literature are ones which concern themselves primarily with the work's beauty and form, rather than with extra-textual issues such as politics or **context**. Aesthetics, which involves the exploration of beauty and nature in literature and the fine arts, involves two theoretical approaches: (a) the philosophical study of the nature and definition of beauty; and (b) the psychological examination of the perceptions, origins and performative effects of beauty.

Aetiology—From Greek words *aitita* meaning cause, and *logos*, meaning rational discourse, aetiology is the philosophical or scientific pursuit of laws of cause and effect.

Affective fallacy—Term coined by W. K. Wimsatt and M. C. Beardsley, which identifies the mistaken analysis of a text in terms of its emotional or 'affective' results, thereby misunderstanding the difference between what a text is and what it does (see **intentional fallacy**).

Aga saga—Largely derisive term, referring to novels such as those by Joanna Trollope and others of a similar kind, usually set in the Home Counties. *Aga* is a proprietary name for a brand of stove that burns solid fuel, gas or oil. The name is an acronym for the original Swedish manufacturers, the Swedish Gas Accumulator Company. The term functions not only in a somewhat pejorative fashion, but also as synecdoche, signifying novels concerned with the largely domestic and occasionally erotic lives of upper-middle class incomers in now gentrified rural communities, the circles of their friends and acquaintances, and the minor intrigues arising from out of such societies.

Agency—Literally 'activeness'; more usually used to suggest one's ability to act on the world on one's own behalf or the extent to which one is empowered to act by the various **ideological** frameworks within which one operates.

Agitprop—Originally a neologism in Russian, combining notions of agitation and propaganda, the term was given to a department of the Central Committee of the Russian Communist party. Subsequently, the term has come to define any such activities by groups or individuals, which activities are aimed at the production of political unrest and the dissemination of political propaganda.

Alienation—In marxist theories, alienation is the experience of being distanced or **estranged** from the products of one's labour, and by extension from one's own sense of **self**, because of the effects of **capitalism**.

Alienation effect—Loose translation of the German *verfremdung-seffekt*, which might somewhat more accurately be translated as 'estrangement effect', the term was first employed by German playwright Bertolt Brecht. He sought to distance and estrange his audiences from his plays by means of an ensemble of devices – projection, banners and signs, exaggerated gestures, voices and performances, on the part of the actors, and the abandonment of naturalistic behaviour and stage sets in general – in order to prohibit humanist empathy or identification with characters or situations in the plays. The purpose was to engage the audience critically, intellectually and ideologically, suspending feeling and inviting judgement, and to reveal the historical and material dimensions of human actions (see **estrangement**).

Allegory—A literary mode involving extended narratives that produce secondary meanings regarding the story that exists on the surface; otherwise, a form of indirect representation (perhaps best summarised as analogical rather than mimetic). Allegory often functions as a delimiting force because it limits the possible spheres of interpretation to its primary analogy. Characters in allegorical works frequently serve as **metaphors** for abstract ideas.

Alterity—Condition of **otherness** in critical and philosophical discourse to signal a state of **being** apprehended as absolutely, radically other. Emmanuel Levinas addresses the absolute exteriority of alterity, as opposed to the **binary**, **dialectic** or reciprocal structure implied in the idea of the other. For Levinas, the face of the other is the concrete figure for alterity. My sense of **self** is interrupted in my encounter with the face of the other, and thus the self, the I as Levinas puts it, knows itself no longer in its self-sameness but in its own alterity, in coming face to face with the face of the other.

Ambiguity—The condition of an utterance having more than one meaning, thereby producing uncertainty. The term is given detailed attention by William Empson whose analysis denotes the richness and variety of verbal speech. Empson's conception of ambiguity includes seven categories: (a) a given word or syntax can connote several effective meanings at once; (b) two or more meanings may comprise a writer's single intended meaning; (c) a pun can offer two simultaneous ideas; (d) a writer can employ different meanings in order to establish a clear, albeit complicated, state of mind; (e) an image may exist halfway between two ideas; (f) readers may be forced to concoct their own interpretations when confronted with contradictory statements by the writer; and (g) two contradictory meanings may signal an intellectual division in the writer's state of mind.

Ambivalence—Conventionally, the term signals powerful mutually contradictory feelings concerning a particular subject or the uncertainty arising from such an unresolved state. Employed in particular strands of postcolonial critical discourse and developed specifically from the work of Homi Bhabha, ambivalence in this **context** signifies the condition produced through the discourse of **mimicry**, whereby in the process of imposing on the colonial subject the desire to render that **subject** the same as the coloniser (for example, through the coloniser's language), there is produced, says Bhabha, a **difference**, slippage or excess. Thus, the colonial other is produced as almost, but not quite, the same, thereby producing disquiet in the colonialist, and thus a renewal of the fear of the other.

Anaclisis—More conventionally presented as adjective, *anaclitic* or in the phrase *anaclitic type*, originally found in Freud, the concept refers to a personality type that fixes another person as its 'love-object', but the fixation is governed by a more primal need, such as hunger. Anaclisis thus refers to a form of libidinal displacement by the subject.

Analogy—From the Greek *ana*, according to, and *logos*, rational discourse: an analogy is a comparison made between one word, object, story or concept and another for purposes of comparison and explanation.

Anamorphosis—From the Greek meaning 'transformation', the term defines distorted projection effects in works of art, applied to particular objects. When viewed from a conventional perspective the particular object is unintelligible; it makes no sense within the representational image as a whole. When viewed from a different perspective, the image assumes proper proportions, and its identity becomes intelligible. Perhaps the most famous example of an anamorphic object occurs in Hans Holbein's *The Ambassadors*: what appears to be a yellowish or ivory coloured smear across the floor of the room in which the Ambassadors stand, when viewed from one side is revealed as a skull, and thus understood symbolically as a *memento mori*, a reminder of human mortality.

Anaphora—From the Greek meaning 'to carry back', this is a rhetorical device whereby a phrase or word is repeated in successive clauses. Alternatively, *anaphora* is a grammatical term indicating a word that supplements a preceding word or group of words; for example, the use of *he* or *she* following the initial use of the proper name.

Analytical criticism—Type of criticism which assumes the text or other work of art as an organic or autonomous whole, the meaning of which can be discerned without reference to features supposedly external to the text (e.g. **context**, history, **ideology**) through close consideration of its various features and their formal relationships within the work.

Anastomosis—Originally a biological term indicating interconnection between blood vessels, but given a literary application by J. Hillis Miller who points out a contradiction within the etymology and definition of anastomosis: it suggests an intercommunication between, on the one hand, 'two vessels' and, on the other, 'two channels'. Furthermore, the figure of anastomosis is doubly contradictory, in that it figures, as Miller puts it, both 'container and thing contained'. As preface to a lengthy critical analysis of Goethe's *Elective Affinities*, Miller examines James Joyce's own use of the word. Joyce employs the term three times, once in *Ulysses* and twice in *Finnegans Wake*. As Miller shows, anastomosis for Joyce marks: (a) the interconnection between past, present, and future; (b) the interconnection of 'each person to all the previous generations back to Adam and Eve; (c) the 'intercommunication' of sexual intercourse; and (d) the intercommunication imagined in the passing of 'the genetic message on to future generations'.

Androgyny—A perceived or projected ambiguity or indeterminacy with regard to a person's gender or sexual identity. To be androgynous is, on the one hand, to have characteristics of both male and female. In mythological narratives or paintings based on myth or **allegory** this can be represented through the appearance of both male and female physical attributes, or simply in a facial physiognomy whereby it is impossible to tell whether one is looking at a man or a woman, while to the eye there is intimation of both. On the other hand, to be androgynous is to appear as neither specifically masculine or feminine, according to a specific culture's dominant models, constructions, or discourses pertaining either to masculinity or femininity. The condition of androgyny is not simply governed by perception or the analytical judgment of an audience. It can be staged or performed strategically so as to disrupt or obscure, or otherwise draw attention to the constricting aspect of societally normative gender roles.

Angry young man—The phrase was first used in 1956, largely by journalists, following the premiere of John Obsborne's play *Look Back in Anger*. Subsequently adopted by critics, the phrase rapidly passed into a broader use to define both rebellious, often working-class male characters in plays and novels (to which the phrase 'kitchen sink drama' was also applied), and also novelists such as Alan Sillitoe and playwrights such as Osborne, who were either from working-class backgrounds or who wrote about working-class themes (or what the *Times Literary Supplement* described in 1957, somewhat pompously, as 'proletarian artistry'). Perhaps somewhat misunderstood and defined retrospectively as a movement (it was never this cohesive), the 'angry young man' was also given expression in social realist cinema in England in the early to mid-1960s by film-makers such as

Lindsay Anderson, Tony Richardson and Karel Reisz; in documentaries such as *We Are the Lambeth Boys*; or feature films such as *Saturday Night and Sunday Morning, A Kind of Loving,* or *The Loneliness of the Long Distance Runner.*

Anthropologism—From the Greek *anthropos*, human, and *logos*, rational discourse: anthropology is the science of humanity; by extension, anthropologism is the application of anthropological insights, methods and practices to other fields of intellectual engagement.

Anthropomorphism—The transformation of a non-human **subject** through an analysis which imbues with qualities peculiar to human beings and thereby makes familiar or 'quasi-human' the subject in question.

Antifoundationalism—Term that refers to the rejection of the philosophy of the existence of a single, unified whole in which everything is ultimately interrelated. Divided into three principal subcategories – sophism, pragmatism and scepticism – antifoundationalism underscores the notion that knowledge is transient and is commonly derived from personal experience.

Anti-intentionalism—A critical position in which the intentions of the author are regarded as immaterial to the interpretation of the work.

Antimaterialist—Any critical or theoretical stance which opposes a materialist viewpoint; that is, any stance that refuses the conditions of material life as the basis of its interpretation. Antimaterialism can be mystical or religious, or it can simply be a depoliticised position.

Anxiety of influence—Concept developed by Harold Bloom in his book of the same name. Bloom's phrase signals a theory of poetic influence and indebtedness. Specifically, Bloom's theory addresses the way in which the work of major, or what Bloom calls 'strong', poets persists as an influence on poets of later ages, and how later poets, in developing and struggling with their strong precursors, effectively 'misread' their influences so as to produce their own 'strong' poetry. The process of struggling with one's major influences, Bloom argues, involves inescapable 'anxieties of indebtedness'.

Aporia/aporetic—Deriving from the Greek for 'unpassable path' or 'impasse', aporia has been used by Jacques Derrida to describe the effects of *différance*: the aporetic and the experience of its excess is figured in the **undecidable** in meaning; irreducible to a limited semantic horizon, language announces its radical undecidability, whereby contrary to the limits of logic, a concept is shown to be identifiable as being disturbed internally, on the one hand, as *neither* this *nor* that, while, on the other hand, as *both* this *and* that.

Archaeology—Term used by Michel Foucault which indicates a mode of analysis or methodology of discursive formations and statements without assigning or seeking origins in the human sciences (e.g. psychiatry, political economy). For Foucault, such discursive strands or strata, those subject-specific languages embedded in a particular culture, distinguish the human sciences from any 'pure' scientificity in that they invoke **ideologies**, beliefs and interests beyond any statement of disinterested data.

Arche-écriture—From the Greek, *arche* means a founding, original or governing, controlling principle; Jacques Derrida coins the term, translatable as archi- or archewriting, to indicate how the very idea of an origin or founding principle is not self-sufficient, full or undifferentiated but, at its origin, is always already traced by the work of **différance** or **writing** in order for it to be articulated. Sense or meaning is never originary or fully present but always spaced and structured temporally.

Archetype—Chiefly in the psychoanalytic theory of Carl Jung and the literary criticism of Northrop Frye, archetypes are those pervasive or supposedly universal symbols that recur from culture to culture and transhistorically. For Jung, the archetype is a primordial image that recurs throughout human civilisation in various forms, always referring back to the original type. For Frye, archetypes are symbols that recur recognisably from one literary text to another, and across otherwise disparate literary forms, genres and cultures.

Architectonic—Referring to construction or structure and, as Aristotle employs it, having control over structure, the term is used critically as addressing the systematisation of knowledge.

Archive—Originally either a public office or building in which documents were stored, or the historical documents making up an archive as a form of public or social memory, the term also operates as a verb to indicate the activity of archiving, of preserving documents, records and so on. In computing terms, archiving refers to the hierarchical storing of infrequently used files or documents. Generally, archiving refers to the storing of any data, whether materially or virtually. In *Archive Fever*, Jacques Derrida offers analysis of the notion of the archive in relation to particular Freudian concepts concerning memory and what Freud perceived as the hierarchical embedding of memories in the conscious and unconscious. Additionally, Derrida speculates on the effects of virtual storage (on the internet, hypertext, and so on) on the idea of the archive and the possible transformation or *spectralisation* of the notion of the archive and archiving.

Aristotelian—Ideas deriving from the writings of Aristotle, whose *Poetics* in particular is an early example of literary criticism. The *Poetics* is an analysis of the elements of tragedy that make one example of the genre more or less successful than another example. His focus is on the structure of the plot, especially as it connects to the moral lesson of the play. He isolates the features that have since come to be known as the unities: the unities of time (the action takes place in one day), place (it takes place in one location) and action (it is concerned with one significant action). The highest shape of the tragic plot in Aristotle's terms was one which focused on elements of reversal in the fortunes of the protagonists, recognitions of moral lessons and catharsis in the audience whereby the viewer is purged by his or her experience of seeing the action played out. The emphasis is thereby on structure and the audience's moral response to structure.

Aura—Providing aesthetic theory with an important critical term Walter Benjamin's concept of the 'aura' of a work of art is what Benjamin calls the 'unique phenomenon of distance' that is to be found in high cultural forms. The term refers to matters of an artwork's uniqueness and authenticity. While the auratic places an artwork beyond the quotidian, for Benjamin reproductions create a plurality of copies where there was once a unique existence. Benjamin also notes the auratic in natural objects, while insisting, in both the artwork and the natural object, the experience of the auratic as the experience of a falling away, a decaying or disappearance always already in process. The auratic, it should be noted, is not figured nostalgically, even though the artwork's aura appears to be threatened by 'mechanical reproduction' or, as Samuel Weber more accurately translates it, 'technological reproducibility', which in principle dissipates the work's uniqueness or singularity. The unique artefact is distanced by its uniqueness in a weave of both space and time. However, Benjamin argues that, though dissipated by modern technologies of reproduction, a work's aura continues to give it **authority** and mystery.

Auteur theory—Developed as an explanatory notion by contributors to the film studies journal *Cahiers du Cinéma* regarding the control the director has over the making of a film, from questions of diegesis, narrative, editing, framing and so on. An 'auteur' (Fr. 'author') is a director whose vision is assumed to be recognisable stylistically and rhetorically across a range of films. Thus, arguably, the movies of Woody Allen or Ingmar Bergman have recognisable elements, motifs, concerns, repeated edits, shots and so on which, from film to film, are elements of the film maker's 'signature'.

Author/authorship—The notion of authorship refers to the concept of the individual who employs his or her imaginative and intellectual powers in the construction of a given literary text, while, historically, concepts of authorship have been tied to the legal status of creative works and the rights of the author. In the poststructuralist era, the idea of authorship has become dispersed or radically rethought. Many literary theorists, for example, subscribe to the concept of authorship as the product of multiple cultural, historical and social forces that impact the act of textual production. Hence, Roland Barthes announced the 'death of the author' in 1968 in an effort to challenge our existing, traditional notions of authorship and textual authority.

Authorial intention—The idea that, through the close reading of a literary text, the reader can discern or in some manner gain access to the author's intentions, or what the author really means to say.

Authority—The power that comes from the assumption of being unique or originary, or the significance invested in the cultural status of an originator or author (from which the word derives) of a given work; the assumption of power invested in signs, practices, laws or discursive practices. Thus, the limits placed on meaning when interpreters turn to the biographies or the known **authorial intentions**.

Autonomy of art—The view that art/literature is autonomous – that is, that it has no function beyond itself, that it is politically, socially, economically and personally disengaged; a view of literature favoured, implicitly or explicitly by the New Critics in the US, and by F. R. Leavis and the other contributors to *Scrutiny*.

Avant-garde—From the French for 'vanguard', avant-garde in art or literature means artistic practices the deviate daringly from conventional practice: the art of the new.

| B |

Bad faith—This phrase occurs first in French as *mauvaise foi* in Jean-Paul Sartre's *Being and Nothingness*. Developing his concept of being in response to Heideggerian and Husserlian notions of consciousness and being, and considering ideas of human freedom, Sartre applies the term to the appropriation of a false notion of selfhood on the part of human consciousness. For him, bad faith is not a condition imposed on consciousness by the world, but a willingness on the part of the individual to accept conditions of existence in the face of what, for Sartre, is clearly faulty or in error. To provide a perhaps oversimplified example of living in bad faith, it might be argued that one has a false consciousness of one's being by perceiving oneself through what one does. When asked the ontological question, 'who are you?', a reply of 'I am a teacher' or 'I am a writer' would be a bad-faith expression of one's self.

Base/Superstructure—Concepts derived from Marx's Preface to *A Contribution to the Critique of Political Economy*. Marx argued that the economic organisation of any given society (what he called the relations of production or Base) was the foundation of all other social relations and cultural production: that is, the economic Base makes possible or determines the kinds of legal, political, religious and general cultural life of the world – what Marx termed the Superstructure. The relationship between Base and Superstructure has variously been understood as absolutely determining (the Base is like the foundations for a Superstructure like a house), or as mutually dependent (with the Base acting like railway tracks and the Superstructure as rolling stock). In early marxist models the relationship between base and superstructure is seen as static, the latter being supposedly a **reflection** of the former. This model is replaced by a more mobile understanding premised on **mediation**.

Becoming–In the context of modern literary theory, **being** is both spatial and temporal, perceived as an event implying relationship to others and as a process of continuity or becoming. The concept of becoming is articulated in the work of Gilles Deleuze and Félix Guattari in relation to the economics and **flow** of desire. Because the flow of desire precedes the **subject**, such flow is neither restricted to nor defined in relation to the psyche of the individual. Traversing subjectivity, flows open onto potential becomings. Because the notion of becoming is indicative in the work of Deleuze and Guattari of an oceanic, radical destabilisation of discrete or finite meaning or identity (see **deterritorialisation**), it cannot be thought as merely being a liberatory transformation which, once achieved, comes to rest in an alternative identity (such transformation would merely reside within a general process of economic exchange). Indeed, it is because of the radically utopian conceptualisation of becoming as resistant to the very idea of meaning or identity that it becomes problematic in the extreme to provide a definition. Deleuze and Guattari describe a series of different becomings – becoming-animal, becoming-woman, becoming-imperceptible, becoming-minoritarian, **becoming-other** – all of which are examples of the multiplicity of flows termed **desiring machines**. None of these implies a conscious imitation or identification but, in the words of Tamsin Lorraine, 'becomings are encounters that engage the subject at the limits of corporeal and conceptual logics already formed and so bring[ing] on the destabilisation of conscious awareness that forces the subject to a genuinely creative response'. Becoming is thus for Deleuze and Guattari, 'absolute deterritorializations'. 'To become animal', they write (to take one example of the envisioning of becoming) 'is to participate in movement, to stake out a path of escape in all its positivity, to cross a threshold, to reach a continuum of intensities that are valuable only in themselves, to find a world of pure intensities where all forms come undone, as do all the significations, signifiers and signifieds, to the benefit of an unformed matter of deterritorialized flux, of nonsignifying signs' (see **empty signifier**).

Being—In philosophical discourse, the term is applicable to all objects of sense or thought, material or immaterial. In continental philosophy, aspects of being are distinguished in the following ways: (a) as *being-for-(it)self*, which names conscious being or being as actuality; (b) *being-in-(it)self*, this phrase identifying being either which lacks conscious awareness or which otherwise determines being as mere potentiality; (c) *being-itself*, which determines the idea of pure being, regarded as infinite and uncharacterisable, also usually signified as *Being*; (d) *being-with*, which names human existence as part of a shared community of beings. Martin Heidegger has provided the most sustained and radical reorientation of the question of Being in twentieth-century philosophy, employing the term *Dasein* (lit. *there-*

being) to indicate the condition of beings within Being. One's being is a *there-being* in that one only comprehends one's being as 'thrown', to use Heidegger's term. This suggests that being is never experienced in the abstract but only ever in the experience of *being-in-the-world*. Heidegger employs the term *Dasein* in order to move beyond discourses of being rooted in notions of an originary or grounding being from which first principle we might then comprehend our being. Furthermore, the thinking of *Dasein* therefore does not assume intrinsic or essential qualities to being but, instead, conceives being in its temporal existence in relation to others in order to examine the experience of being and how existence is possible. *Dasein* is thus not the expression of a self-reflexive entity reflecting on the world, but is always already immersed in the world, our existence determined through specific historical and cultural locations.

Belles-lettres— French, originally a parallel term to *beaux arts* (fine arts) signifying 'literary studies', the term has now come to be used vaguely and occasionally derisively in referring to the lighter aspects of literary study.

Bildungsroman—From the German, meaning 'education [*bildung*] novel [*roman*]' a novel that traces the formative years and spiritual education of its principal protagonist. *David Copperfield* or *Great Expectations* could be considered English variations on the German model.

Binary opposition—Any pair of terms which appear diametrically opposed; therefore: good/evil, day/night, man/woman, centre/margin. First considered by Aristotle in his *Poetics*, and subsequently given attention much later among structuralist and poststructuralist thinkers. In literary theoretical discourse, neither term in a binary opposition or pair is considered absolute. Rather, one term defines and is, in turn, defined by what appears to be its opposite. As the work of Jacques Derrida shows, any pair of terms, far from maintaining their absolute semantic value, slide endlessly along a semantic chain, the one into the other through the effect of **difference**. Also, Derrida makes clear how the apparent equivalence of terms is not in fact true: instead, in all binary oppositions, one term, usually the former of the two, is privileged hierarchically over the **other** in Western thought.

Black/white—The terms refer to the **racial binaries** that continue to have an impact on the course of Western culture, particularly in terms of identity politics and regarding existing ethnic biases and prejudice.

Blaxploitation—Term signifying action films made mostly in the 1970s, in which African-Americans are principally portrayed as violent, criminal, and sexualised in unrealistic and exploitative, degrading ways.

Bourgeois—French for middle class. By extension, it has come to mean a set of conventional attitudes which tend to support a conservative status quo.

Bourgeois individualism—A key term in Ian Watt's proto-marxist study *The Rise of the Novel*, used to define one of the conditions for the novel's appearance. The bourgeois individual exhibited a new kind of (middle-class) **consciousness**, and new sensibility in relation to his or her relations with God, other people generally and servants in particular, and the market, consisting primarily in a view that the individual is significant in his or her own right, rather than having his or her significance subsumed by the general needs of society.

Bricolage—French term, the equivalent of 'do-it-yourself', it came into use in structuralist criticism in the early 1960s in the work of Claude Lévi-Strauss. Works of art or literature to which the term is applied are understood as being constructed from a diverse range of materials, objects, or intertextual sources; otherwise, the term refers to the act of construction.

| C |

Camp—Camp is notoriously difficult to define but critical considerations such as those of Jonathan Dollimore and Alan Sinfield agree that the question of camp involves an act or performance which, while remaining elusive, nonetheless destabilises the perception of stable gender identity. There is little consensus among critics as to a definition of camp and this it might be suggested is camp's strength. What can be said, albeit cautiously, is that camp appears to be a performative play which engages with flirtation, comedy and flippancy, occasionally, if not frequently, for the purpose of pointed critical attack. There is in camp a glib, self-reflexive admission that what Jonathan Dollimore terms the 'masquerade of camp' shows up the lack of substance in any normative construction of identity. While camp, strictly speaking, is concerned with codes concerning the reading of performance of gender- and sexually orientated identities, the performative condition of camp masquerade for a form of dis-identification within identity – the deliberate staging of a gendered identity announces that all gendered positions are, to some extent, performances without essence – which refuses both to allow itself to be taken seriously and to be pinned down. One cannot fix the notion of an identity-in-common for the idea of camp. Moving between normative and transgressive gendered identities, transgressing the very idea of gender, camp announces the paradoxical power *and* powerlessness instituted in the politics of gender identities.

Canon/canonical/canonicity—Originally, the term *canon* referred to those books of the Bible that had been accepted by Church authorities as containing the word of God. More recently, in literary studies, it has come to mean the 'great books', or 'great tradition' of texts that everyone should study or know in order to be considered educated in literature – that is, works called 'canonical'. The means by which the canon has been constructed, however, have been radically exclusionary – leaving out, for example, works written by those in marginal or excluded groups. Contemporary focus on canonicity, therefore, has tended to move towards broadening the category of what 'counts' as literature.

Capitalism—Any system of economic relations which is driven by the profit motive; capitalism depends on the investment by private individuals and companies of their own funds to provide the economic means of production, distribution and exchange in return for profits from their investment and which typically relies on competition, a free economic market, and private or corporate ownership of the means of production.

Carnival/carnivalesque—Terms drawn from the work of Mikhail Bakhtin on the novel. The carnivalesque is that in **narrative** forms where social hierarchies and **power** structures oriented around positions of 'high' and 'low' are temporarily inverted, often through forms of parody, in order to destabilise and to make comic that which is taken seriously within social order.

Catachresis—From the Greek, meaning 'misuse', in rhetoric, the term is employed to indicate an incorrect use of words. Jacques Derrida describes the founding concepts of **metaphysics** (*logos*, see **logocentrism**) *eidos* (form), *theoria*, and so on) as instances of catachresis rather than **metaphor**. Defining catachresis as a 'violent production of meaning, an abuse which refers to no anterior or proper meaning', he proposes that philosophy in its literariness is catachrestic. He does so through attention to the violent nature of metaphysical concepts in order to stress how there is no proper or natural connection between the terms of metaphysics and some supposed origin. Moreover, Derrida also attempts to transform terms, for example **writing, text, arché-ecriture, supplement, dissemination, différance,** so as to produce in a violent fashion disruptive meanings as 'new forms of catachresis, or what he calls 'monstrous mutation[s] without tradition or normative precedent'.

Cathexis—Given as the translation of Freud's *libidobesetzung*, the concept refers to the mental process of concentrating and channelling the psychic energy of the *libido* as this is manifested in forms such as anxiety, dread, fear and so on. Also the term refers to the displacement of *libidinal* interest to objects.

Chiasmus—A grammatical term referring to the inversion of word order from one clause to another.

Chora—Originally deriving from Plato's *Timaeus*, where the word is a figure of multiple **ambiguity**, meaning 'the receptacle of meaning, invisible and formless, which contains intelligibility but cannot itself be understood'. Jacques Derrida, spelling the term *khora*, provides a telling analysis of Plato's text, in which he aims to demonstrate how *khora* can be defined in ways pertaining neither to the sensible (having to do with feeling and emotion) nor the intelligible (having to do with rationality and intellect), and thus names that which is resistant to naming, which cannot be gathered by any name, and yet which is neither negative nor positive; *khora* thus 'names', if we can put it this way, the **aporetic** beyond, in excess of, any defining paradigm, while being irreducible to a definition as either just this experience of the aporetic or the idea of the **aporia**. Julia Kristeva has adapted the term to describe a pre-linguistic realm which underpins language and meaning, but which cannot itself be pinned down. In the process of language development the chora is split to enable words (defined by limitation – by what they leave out) to come into meaning. The chora represents endless possibility but no single significance – single significance being what defines language itself.

Chronotope—Concept developed by Mikhail Bakhtin, which refers to the aesthetic or envisioning of the human **subject** as situated materially within a specific geotemporal location or spatial/temporal structure which determines the shape of a **narrative**; thus, protagonists of epic narratives can be described as defined by, as well as inhabiting, a particular chronotopic space.

Clinamen—A trope, signifying a swerve. The figure is employed by Harold Bloom to describe the act of poetic misprision by which poets of later generations produce their strong readings of the earlier poets who influence them (see **anxiety of influence**).

Close reading—Formal analysis of the recurrent figures, motifs, tropes of a text so as to suggest a greater unity or organic whole to the work; a term usually associated with new criticism or the work of F. R. Leavis and other critics associated with Leavis and the journal *Scrutiny*. In this sense, close reading is implicitly assumed to be an act of reading divorced from any matters supposedly extraneous to the text, such as **context**, matters of history, questions of politics, issues of gender and race, and so on.

Code—The signification system that allows for the comprehension of a text or event.

Codification—The process of establishing rules and procedures that are apparently consistent and coherent for any intellectual practice. In structuralism, the process of unravelling and interpreting codes of signification – for example, the codes that tell you that this is a detective novel, and that that is an advert for pizza.

Collective unconscious—The idea of a collective unconscious is posited by Carl Jung in *The Archetypes and the Collective Unconscious*. In addition to a personal unconscious, Jung argues that human cultures share a collective and impersonal psychic system, consisting of pre-existent forms, defined by Jung as *archetypes*. Of such forms the subject only becomes conscious when these are given specific personal psychic forms.

Collocation—A linguistic term referring to habitual juxtaposition or arrangement of words in relation to others, or to phrases conventionally associated with one another.

Colonial/colonialism—Terms denoting the manner in which one culture appropriates the land, people and resources of another to further its **imperialist** ends. Edward Said defines colonialism as the necessary consequence of imperialist practices and attitudes, thereby suggesting a causal relationship. As a consequence of colonial occupation and the discourses and practices generated and maintained by colonisers, the idea of colonialism may also be said to designate the attributes of the specific political and **epistemological** discourses by which the colonising power defines those who are subjected to its rule. Postcolonialism refers in literary studies to literary texts produced in countries and cultures that have come under the control of European powers at some point in their history.

Commodification—The process by which an object or a person becomes viewed primarily as an article for economic exchange – or a commodity. Also the translation of the **aesthetic** and cultural objects into principally economic terms. The commodification of an object or the raw materials from which it is produced is a sign of the transformation from **use-value** to **exchange-value**. The term is used in feminist theory to describe the objectification of women by patriarchal cultures. Through the processes of commodification, the work of art lacks any significance unless it can be transformed by economic value into a mystified, desired form, the labour having gone into its production having been occluded.

Commodity fetishism—Term used by marxist critics after Marx's discussion in Volume I of *Capital* to describe the ways in which products within capitalist economies become objects of veneration in their own right, and are valued way beyond what Marx called their 'use-value'. Commodity fetishism is understood as an example of the ways in which social relations are hidden within economic forms of capitalism.

Condensation—A psychoanalytic, specifically Freudian, term referring to the psychic process whereby phantasmatic images assumed to have a common affect are condensed into a single image. Drawing on the linguistic work of Roman Jakobson, Jacques Lacan compares the Freudian notion of condensation to the work of metaphor.

Connotation/denotation—A word's connotations are those feelings, undertones, associations, etc. that are not precisely what the word means, but are conventionally related to it, especially in poetic language such as metaphor. The word gained popular currency in relation to structuralist theories of language and literature, where connotation is opposed to denotation – the precise meaning of a word, what it means exactly as opposed to what it might mean by association. Denotation is the act or process of implying or connoting meaning or ideas.

Consciousness—In Freudian discourse, one of the principal manifestations of the psychic apparatus, the others being the unconscious and preconscious.

Constative speech act—In *How to do Things with Words*, J. L. Austin defines different types of speech act, including *constative* and *performative*. A constative speech act is a statement which can be judged as either true or false, such as 'the sky is blue'. A *performative* is a way of doing things with words, as in the example of a promise, baptising or christening, the naming of ships, or the priest saying 'I now pro-

nounce you man and wife', whereby the words enforce a
social reality within a given and commonly understood
cultural context. According to Austin, performatives cannot
be true or false, only felicitous or infelicitous, so the pro-
nouncement on the part of the priest when uttered in a play,
novel or film is infelicitous. However, this has been extensively and comprehensively brought into question in the
work of Jacques Derrida, who argues that a performative
maintains its force and the possibility of doing something
with words regardless of the context. There are other types of
speech act for Austin. Locutionary acts are, in Austin's
words, 'roughly equivalent to uttering a certain sentence
with a certain "meaning" in the traditional sense'. Illocutionary acts are those which have a certain conventional
force, such as warnings, orders, or speech acts intended to
give information. Perlocutionary acts are those we use to
bring about something, examples of which include persua-
sion or convincing someone of something (see **Speech-act
theory**).

Constellation—The idea of the constellation names for Walter
Benjamin the critical observation of **heterogeneous**, yet not
absolutely dissimilar, images and figures of thought gathered
from both present experience and other historical moments.
Benjamin seeks to maintain the **difference** of the historial
condition of thought, rather than troping figures, concepts
and ideas from the past in terms of present conceptualisation
by some transhistorical critical gesture.

Consumer culture—A description of postwar Western-type
economies in which the consumption of commodities –
and of cultural artefacts as commodities – is a principal
determining feature of a specific society.

Context—Usually used simply to describe all the extra-textual
features (conditions of production and reception, historical
events, general cultural milieu, biography, etc.) which may
have a bearing on the interpretation of a literary text. The
term has also been co-opted and adapted by Luce Irigaray to
describe a kind of **écriture féminine** in which the **analogy**
between pen and penis derived from Freudian thought is

rewritten to an analogy between cunt (in French *con*) and writing, hence *con-texte*.

Co-optation—The process of borrowing from one discourse the methods and theoretical models of another, often with radical effects. Politically, the appropriation of an individual or group, or the ideas of an opposition, and put to work willingly or otherwise in the service of those who effect the appropriation.

Counter-history/counter-memory—Terms employed by Michel Foucault in his critique of psychology's official historical account of the history of madness socially and institutionally conceived. Conventional historical models of **narrative** are grounded in psychological terms of continuity and identity. In contradistinction to such models, Foucault seeks through various reading strategies and the deployment of various concepts to resist any monolithic history of mental illness. Treating the various modalities of discourse at different historical moments, Foucault offers a discontinuous counter-history. In arguing for a disjunctive and polyvocal counter-history which in its consideration of discourse, modes of confinement, surveillance and the psychiatric gaze, for example, gives access to a critical perspective on present views of mental illness through a critical history disruptive of progressivist models, Foucault seeks to constitute a counter-memory, that which is forgotten in the official and institutional 'memory' expressed as the history of psychology or psychiatry.

Countertransference—Psychoanalytic term, coined by Freud but employed to a far greater extent after his death by other analysts, to indicate the analyst's unconscious emotions towards the analysand. Lacan reformulates the idea of countertransference in terms of resistance, a structural dynamic typical of the analytic experience, and grounded in a fundamental incommensurability between **desire** and speech.

Critical Theory—Critical Theory has at least two definitions. At its narrowest or most specific, it is the term used to define the largely marxist influenced and oriented work of the principal members of the Institute for Social Research of Frankfurt University, founded in 1924, notably, Theodor Adorno,

Max Horkheimer, Herbert Marcuse, and Jürgen Habermas, whose work is otherwise generally and collectively known by the name 'Frankfurt School'. More generally, critical theory is also a term assumed to be roughly synonymous with, or is otherwise substituted for the equally nebulous, and potentially vacuous phrase, 'literary theory'. The term has come to signify a constellation or loose amalgam of contemporary approaches to textual (literary or filmic) and cultural criticism, for example structuralism, semiotics or poststructuralism. Such discourses are central to much critical work in English studies, comparative literature and cultural studies. At the same time, recent interdisciplinary developments have meant that such approaches are being considered and applied in other disciplines, as diverse as history, theology and law. Many of the ideas and theorists arose in the intellectual environments of France and Germany. The breadth (or, more negatively, the emptiness or uselessness) of the term is immediately comprehended if one considers that, amongst others, Derrida and deconstruction, negative theology and ecocriticism, modernism and postmodernism, as well as the Frankfurt School, along with the work of Levinas, Blanchot and Lacoue-Labarthe are all readily appropriated under this definition within institutions of higher education throughout the English-speaking world. Critical theory thus becomes, it might be said, a definition for a variety of critical praxes for which there is no other homogenising determination.

Criticism—The act of analysing and evaluating literary texts, films and images, cultural forms and phenomena. The varieties of criticism are numerous and extend at least as far back as Aristotle's *Poetics*.

Cultural capital—A phrase used by Pierre Bourdieu to describe the hidden value attached to learning and education in otherwise apparently ruthlessly capitalist Western societies; also, the dissemination of literary knowledge for the express purpose of enhancing the moral sensibilities of a given nation or culture's readership.

Cultural materialism—A term first associated with marxist critic Raymond Williams that refers to the manner in which economic forces and modes of production inevitably impinge upon cultural products such as literary works. Movement in British literary theory that insistently pursues the materialist basis of cultural phenomena. Alongside textual evidence, cultural materialists pursue all kinds of contextual evidence in order to try to explain the text as a material object – both an object produced at a particular time, and an object being consumed in the present.

Cultural poetics—Term first employed by Stephen Greenblatt in 1988, to signify a mode of critical analysis developed upon the premises of new historicism, but distinct from it. The analytical praxis of a cultural poetics concerns the identification of historically and culturally distinct cultural practices as these arise in particular historical moments, and the relations between the practices and the discourses by which they are articulated.

Culture—The patterns of human knowledge that refer to the customary beliefs, social formations and traits of racial, religious or social groups. Culture similarly denotes an acquaintance with the humanities, fine arts and other intellectual or scientific pursuits. The term culture is applied to assemblages of social practices defined periodically and in terms of race, belief and class.

Cyberwar—Term often associated with Paul Virilio that refers to the commodification of information and its nearly invisible dispersal within technological culture. Cyberwar entails virtual enemies inflicting virtual casualties among their invisible foes.

Cyborg—Term used by feminist theorist Donna Haraway to posit an alternative mode of being which, in being a hybrid of human and mechanical elements, would be beyond the constraints of biological sex and culturally stereotyped gender.

D

Dasein—A conventional word in German, given particular significance in phenomenological discourse by Martin Heidegger. The word is a portmanteau word, combining *da* (there) and *Sein* (being). Heidegger uses the word to signify the groundedness of being, the fact of our being-in-the-world and the fact that the subject perceives his or her being as a material condition of existence, rather than apprehending the condition of consciousness from a reflection on an abstract or metaphysical notion of Being. One particular aspect of *Dasein* is that, in common with other beings, the subject comes to apprehend and reflect on the temporality of his or her being; that is, that one's being is always a being-towards-death.

Death drive—Freudian concept concerning human desire to return to a state of non-conflictual stasis, equilibrium or lifelessness. Intensified misdirection of the death drive in terms of psychic internalisation is hypothesised as producing masochism, while direction towards another can result in sadism.

Death of the author—From Roland Barthes's essay of the same title ([1968] 1977), the phrase has come to mean the resistance to using information derived from the writer's life or known **authorial intentions** as part of the process of interpretation since this presumes that the author imposes the final limit on meaning and attributes to him (or her) a godlike status.

Deconstruction—Deconstruction is conventionally understood as a school or method of criticism. Equally conventionally, when thought of as a school, method or critical 'programme', deconstruction is understood to have been developed by French philosopher Jacques Derrida. According to conventional narratives, Derrida's 'method' of reading, which apparently sought to unearth contradictions and paradoxes in the logical structures of philosophical and literary texts, became adopted in North American universities from the late 1960s and in British universities from the early 1980s.

However, all such narratives pertaining to deconstruction are wide of the mark in their efforts at definition on several counts. First, it has been assumed that Derrida coins the term 'deconstruction', and that it is therefore a neologism. This is inaccurate, and, as Derrida has, himself, pointed out, it is a very old French word. Furthermore, as the OED shows, the word exists in English, and pre-exists Derrida and other critics' use of the term. Derrida used the word in an effort to 'translate' German philosopher Martin Heidegger's use of the words 'destruktion' and 'abbau', in order to demonstrate that which exists within or inhabits in a certain fashion any structure or the idea of any structure by which the articulation of that structure is made possible, and yet which is heterogeneous to the self-identity of the structure, whether one is talking of a conceptual, logical, discursive, institutional or philosophical formation. Because that which is deconstructive is thus internal to the very idea of structure, and yet not definable within the logic of the self-same by which ideas, concepts and beliefs maintain their 'truth' or significance, it is therefore not generalisable as a 'theory' of structure, or structure's internal contradictions. It also therefore follows, as J. Hillis Miller has put it, that because every example of deconstruction differs from every other example, it cannot be transformed or translated into a method of reading or a programme for critical analysis, much less into a set of rules available for use by a so-called 'school' of deconstructive criticism. For these and other reasons, it is problematic, to say the least, to define deconstruction, except by a negative process which moves cautiously by speaking, at least provisionally and in the first instance, of what deconstruction is not.

It does have to be said, however, as a cautionary caveat, that even this is fraught, for as Derrida points out, to define deconstruction either in terms of 'deconstruction is' or 'deconstruction is not' is to rely on an **ontological** procedure which ascribes to 'deconstruction' a 'thingness', an objectivity and identity available to definition and awaiting patiently the ontological delimitation of the term. As Derrida seeks to explain, deconstruction always already takes place in structures, makes their existence and their transformation possible, and is thus patently neither that which is applied in the name of reading nor some formalist exercise in determining how something is put together but is, instead, of political and philosophical import, if not directly political per se, because that which is deconstructive is precisely that in any formation, whether discursive or institutional, which we overlook, which we pass over in silence. In Derrida's words, deconstruction, if it is anything, is an 'economic concept designating the production of differing/deferring'.

Defamiliarisation—A concept employed by Russian formalists, defamiliarisation signifies the attribute of some kinds of writing or other works of art which communicates in non-transparent ways that make the world seem strange. The point of defamiliarisation is that it shakes up reading and writing habits, undercuts conventional propriety in language and literature, and thus prevents the reader from making merely habitual or conventional responses.

Demystification—Term often associated with philosophies of cultural materialism that maintain that only social contradictions and economic conditions, rather than literary criticism and theory, possess the capacity for altering the course of reality; hence, materialist philosophy attempts to 'demystify' **bourgeois** pretensions toward totality and completeness. Alternatively, demystification refers to critical praxis which aims to bring to consciousness the hidden modes of produciton, the labour relations and division of labour, which combine to produce material objects as commodities.

Desire—An ineluctable force in the human psyche distinguished from need, desire holds a crucially central position in Lacanian psychoanalysis and, subsequently, in psychoanalytically inflected critical discourses. Desire for Lacan is always an **unconscious** drive, conscious articulations of desire being merely symptomatic of this unstoppable force. Need is seen as a purely biological instinct, while desire, a purely psychic phenomenon, is a surplus or excess beyond all articulation of demand. Desire, writes Lacan, comes always from the unconscious, and is thus unlocatable as such, while being, equally, 'desire for something else' (as it is expressed in *Ecrits* ([1966] (1977)), by which formula Lacan indicates that one cannot desire what one has, while what is desired is always displaced, deferred.

Desiring machine—Rethinking the processes of desire as these have been defined within psychoanalytic discourse as a function of the human **subject**, Deleuze and Guattari describe desire as machinic. In doing so, they are not seeking to supply an estranging metaphor. Instead, they see the **flow** of **desire** as simply an endless and unstoppable 'flight'. It has no organising or generative organic centre or origin. Nor does desire arise as some function of the self. Desire is subject to no law and the comprehension of the desiring machine serves to **deterritorialise** those forms of thinking which apply to some law or identity. The subject does not produce desire but the flow of desire plays a role in the constitution of the subject.

Determinism—Doctrine maintaining that acts of will, natural occurrences or social phenomena find their origins in preceding events or the laws of nature.

Deterritorialisation—Term often associated with Gilles Deleuze and Félix Guattari that refers to a simultaneous process of fictionalisation, escape from stable states, contiguity, and bifurcation. This process is marked by an eschewing of monolithic ideologies in favour of 'disjunctive syntheses' that allow for genuine interconnection. Moreover, the purpose of deterritorialisation as the pursuit or liberation of what Deleuze and Guattari call **flows** or 'lines of flight' is to destabilise the finite idea of corporeality, the **subject** or the state in potential processes of constant **becoming**.

Diachronic/synchronic—Terms often associated with Ferdinand de Saussure that account for the relationships that exist between phonemes, which he explained in terms of their synchronic and diachronic structures. A phoneme exists in a diachronic, or horizontal, relationship with other phonemes that precede and follow it. Synchronic relationships refer to a phoneme's vertical associations with the entire system of language from which individual utterances derive their meaning.

Dialectic—Broadly speaking, argument whereby truth is arrived at by exposing contradictions in debate; systematic analysis. A term associated with Marxism, derived from the work of G. W. F. Hegel, indicating both a scientific method and the rules of antagonism governing the historical transformations of reality. The Hegelian dialectic is defined, at its simplest, as *thesis – antithesis – synthesis*. In marxist discourse dialectic is the process of change effected by historically opposed forces.

Dialectical materialism—Marxist theory that postulates that material reality exists in a constant state of struggle and transformation, prioritising matter over mind. The three laws of dialectical materialism stress: (a) the transformation from quantity to quality making possible revolutionary change; (b) the constitution of material reality as a unity composed of opposites; (c) the negation of the two oppositions in the condition of material reality, as a result of their antagonism, out of which historical development takes place which, however, still retains traces of the negated elements.

Dialogism—Term derived from the work of Mikhail Bakhtin, indicating the polyphonic play of different voices or discourses in a text, without the assumption of a dominant, monolithic authorial position or voice.

Diaspora—Settling of various peoples away from their homelands; often associated with the notion of the Jewish diaspora in modern Israel, but extended in cultural studies, postcolonial studies and race theory to consider the displacement of peoples by means of force, such as slavery.

Diegesis—A long disused term, brought back into use by film theorists, and subsequently used by Roland Barthes and Gérard Genette, among others, denoting narration or description presented without judgement or analysis.

Différance—Neologism coined by Jacques Derrida. Derrida makes the term differ from the more conventional 'difference' by spelling it with an 'a'. The purpose is to point out that there is that in writing which escapes aural comprehension ('a' in the French pronunciation sounding the same as 'e' in 'différence'). Thus, the difference in 'différance' is purely graphic. In this manner, Derrida signifies the graphic element in the production of meaning, whereby writing silently inscribes the spacing, the deferral and differentiation (both terms implied in 'différance'), spatial and temporal, without which no writing or reading is possible.

Difference—A concept deriving from the political necessity to recognise that different groupings (female people, Black people, gay and lesbian people) differ not only from the white heterosexual norm favoured by Enlightenment thought, but also differ among themselves: women, for example, may be middle-class or working-class, black or chicana, straight or gay or bi, and/or any combination of any set of attributes. Also, the understanding in Saussurian linguistics and structuralist criticism of the way meaning is neither intrinsic to a word nor produced solely through reference to a **signified** or object, but in and through the differential relation to other *signifiers*.

Differenciation—Term often associated with Gilles Deleuze that refers to the increasingly diffuse boundaries between art, technology, industry and society. No longer functioning as obvious demarcations, these boundaries endlessly merge with one another in mass culture. Deleuze develops the term to signify the process of **becoming**-different (which is signalled in the 'c' in the spelling) as the possibility of diversity.

Digitality—Term often associated with Jean Baudrillard that refers to the transformation of human consciousness via mass culture's dissemination in a digital format, otherwise referred to by Baudrillard as the digital logic of the code. When images, thoughts and ideas become disembodied from their creative sources, traditional conceptions such as authorship become diffuse. As Baudrillard suggests, with the ever-increasing destabilisation, loss of reference and semantic finality, resemblance and designation in modes of communication, signs, becoming digital and programmatic in their functions, have only 'tactical' value in relation to other signs.

Dirty realism—A genre of fiction, the definition of which is attributed to the journal *Granta*. It is perceived as a relatively recent movement among North American, chiefly US, writers who produce unembellished, spare narratives of the underbelly of American society.

Discourse—A discussion focused on a specific subject, discourse is defined by Michel Foucault as language practice: that is, language as it is used by various constituencies (the law, medicine, the church, for example) for purposes to do with **power** relationships between people.

Displacement—Freudian term for psychic process whereby one psychic figure is relocated in another manifestation or image. Lacan likens the work of metonymy to displacement.

Dissemination—Term employed by Jacques Derrida. Derrida points up the homophonic similarity between the Latin *semen* and the Greek *sema*, the former signifying 'seed', the latter 'sign', and accords a certain equivalence between the concept of *dissemination* and his radical extension of the notion of writing. This is exemplified in the graphic *sem* of *dissemination*. While there is no necessary relation between the Greek or Latin words, and while utterance supposedly helps determine through **context** the appropriate signification in writing and as the effect of writing, it is impossible to keep in place or otherwise limit the graphic play. Derrida employs the figure of dissemination in opposition to ideas of communication or polysemy. Far from being either fully, unequivocally communicative in a stable, fixed fashion, or being determined by an agreed multiplicity of signification the effects of writing displace decidable signification through excess and overflow ungovernable, as Derrida makes clear, by any concept of communication. However, the term is not negative. Derrida insists that dissemination is affirmative in that it insists on both the multiplicity and heterogeneity of meaning, irrecuperable within any semantic horizon.

Dominant/residual/emergent—Marxist terms derived from the writings of Raymond Williams to describe the ways in which there are competing discourses, beliefs and practices in any given culture. Roughly speaking, the dominant discourses are those to which the majority subscribe at a particular historical moment; the residual are those which persist from the past in presently prevailing ideologies; and the emergent are those discourses which are emerging in a culture, but which have yet to achieve consensus across the majority of the population.

Dream work—The psychic process that translates the latent content of the unconscious into the manifest content comprised of dream images. Two processes by which dream work occurs are *condensation* and *displacement.*

Drive—Term associated with Freudian discourse, and a translation of the German *Trieb*, more usually translated into English as 'instinct'. The two principal drives for Freud are the libidinal and the death drive (see **libido** and **death drive**).

Dromology—Term associated with the work of urbanist and architect, Paul Virilio, from the Greek, *dromos*, for *race*, relating to speed. The term is methodological in orientation, coined by Virilio within a discourse of urban, cultural analysis, which, in being a neologism, serves the strategic purpose of disrupting the commonsensical, while being applied, as an analytical methodology to explore and express cultural and, particularly, urban matters of flow and speed, whether by this Virilio means the speed and acceleration of information transferral through the various modes of tele-technologies, or the question of the accelerated flow of living brought about by transport systems.

E

Ecriture féminine—'Feminine/female writing' (French). Term derived from the writings of Hélène Cixous to describe a mode of textual production that resists dominant **phallic** models of communication. It is not necessarily written by women, but is produced instead by those who occupy what might be called a 'feminine' space in culture – which will often be women, but might also include certain kinds of excluded men.

Ecriture/écrivance—In Roland Barthes' conception, the former is the term for literary writing, that is language which draws attention to its artificiality; the latter term, Barthes contends, signifies that kind of writing, as in realist **narrative**, which strives for transparency, thereby being complicit with the prevailing **dominant ideology**.

Ego—The fundamental, conscious component of the **self**, particularly in terms of the way in which humans contrast themselves with the world. In psychoanalytic theory, the ego functions as one of the three divisions of the psyche and refers to the manner in which people **mediate**, perceive or adapt to reality.

Embodiment—The state of giving body to or becoming incarnate. Also employed to signify an exemplary physical expression of metaphysical values.

Empiricism—Philosophical approach to knowledge which puts forward the idea that all knowledge is derived from experience and not derived from reason or logic.

Empty signifier—Term often associated with Félix Guattari, also given as 'a-signifying' or 'non-signifying', that denotes a **signifier** with a vague, unspecifiable, or non-existent **signified**. In such instances, the signifier has endured a form of radical disconnection from its signified.

Enlightenment—Term used to designate the thought and aims of French philosophers of the eighteenth century.

Epic—Usually a poetic, or occasionally prose, composition in which the heroic exploits of one character or a small group of characters are delineated in a single continuous narrative.

Epic theatre—A style of dramaturgy developed primarily in both practice and theory by Bertolt Brecht from the 1920s onwards. Epic theatre is episodic rather than dramatically unified; it intersperses action with songs, poetry and dance, and it focuses the audience's attention on the fictionality of what they are observing in order to **demystify ideological** modes of production.

Episteme—The idea of the episteme constitutes for Michel Foucault the basis of a possible science of Western culture at specific historical instances. Foucault employs the term 'episteme' to define the constellation of discourses that come together in a particular historical period as the knowledge peculiar to that epoch. Each body of knowledge, while being made up of competing, if not heterogeneous modes of information, is, in effect, a model or structure governing all knowledge, its relationships and communications at a given moment. However, the various forms and articulations of knowledge in a given epoch are not simply intellectual for

Foucault, they are also cultural and, therefore, political. Foucault seeks to express through the idea of the episteme the tensions and relationships between, as he puts it, 'the knowledge of living beings, the knowledge of the laws of language, and the knowledge of economic facts'. For Foucault, it is the function of the historian of ideas, to disentangle the various discourses which constitute the episteme, as though these were so many layers constituting an epoch, hence his use of the figure of archaeology so as to indicate the various sedimented strata of knowledge, which are themselves discontinuous between epochs.

Epistemology—Branch of philosophy which addresses the grounds and forms of knowledge. Michel Foucault employs the idea of the episteme to indicate a particular group of knowledges and discourses which operate in concert as the dominant discourses in any given historical period. He also identifies epistemic breaks, radical shifts in the varieties and deployments of knowledge for ideological purposes, which take place from period to period.

Epoché—Philosophical concept, first encountered in Greek scepticism and subsequently in phenomenology. *Epoché* names the principal of the suspension of judgement in any encounter with undecidability. In phenomenological discourse, assuming the epoché, the subject sets aside all factual, historical or empirical knowledge in order to apprehend phenomena and one's consciousness of them.

Epistolary novel—A novel form, popular in the eighteenth century, the narrative of which is presented through a succession of letters, often between different characters – as in Samuel Richardson's *Clarissa* or Tobias Smollett's *The Expeditions of Humphrey Clinker*.

Erasure—The gesture of erasure, or placing a term under erasure, refers graphically to the act of crossing out a word but retaining the word and the crossing through. Martin Heidegger employs this practice in *The Question of Being* in which the word **Being** is crossed through. Heidegger's purpose is to show how the term can no longer be employed, given that the concept as it is used has slipped away from, and thereby forgotten, the question of Being. For Heidegger, the very idea of Being is always presupposed. Any question asking 'what is "Being"' is only articulable to the extent that the very idea of Being makes it possible to consider the being of Being. But it is this idea which has been occluded in the consideration of Being. Crossing through the word releases it, both from the assumptions that the term is known or that the meaning of Being is somehow understood and the idea that, in asking the question, 'what is "Being"', there is somehow the presumption of an answer. Moreover, as Derrida points out, with regard to Heidegger's practice, the crossing through is not a negative gesture but one which indicates how, while signification is necessary, the thought of the idea of Being as a 'transcendental signified' has reached a particular limit in the text of Heidegger. Derrida also places particular terms *sous rature* (under erasure) because their conventional function within metaphysical and logical discourse is exhausted. Such terms no longer retain their full sense; neither do they signify a presence or origin, for which the signifier stands, but only other structural traces, such as themselves.

Essentialism/essentialist—An essentialist belief is one that mistakenly confuses the effects of biology with the effects of culture; in particular it refers to the belief that biology is more significant than culture in **subject** formation. It is often used as a term of disapproval by critics.

Estrangement—Like **defamiliarisation**, estrangement is a process of making one's experience of text or artwork strange or, more particularly, distant. Its aim is usually to subvert the reading experience (or viewing experience in the visual arts, theatre and film) away from conventions and habits. Sometimes given as a translation for the Brechtian term *Verfremdung*, which is more commonly translated as *alienation*. In the context of Brechtian theatre, estrangement names the theatrical practices by which the audience are encouraged to engage intellectually and ideological with the political and philosophical issues of a play by the deliberate foregrounding of theatrical artifice, thereby seeking to prohibit the audience's engaging empathetically with the subject material or the characters.

Ethics—A set of moral principles or values, as well as an understanding of moral duty and obligation. Ethics also refers to accepted standards of conduct. In literary theory, ethical critics address the moral properties inherent in literary works in an effort to understand their social, cultural or **aesthetic** implications for readers and texts alike.

Ethnicity—Refers to a given individual's racial, national, cultural, religious, tribal or linguistic background, classification or affiliation.

Ethnocentrism—Term designating the cultural analytic by which other cultures are judged, read or interpreted according to the implicit or explicit assumption of the centrality, superiority or primacy of one's own culture. Ethnocentrism has been most visible historically in Northern European attitudes towards non-European cultures, or otherwise in the cultural assumptions made by technologically advanced cultures, particularly those of the Northern Hemisphere towards those cultures not so technologically developed. Similarly, historically ethnocentrism has manifested itself in colonial and religious or quasi-religious contexts, whereby colonising and invading forces have assumed non-white and/or non-Christian cultures to be barbaric, 'heathen', or, in some instances, not human. Ethnocentrist attitudes thus transform relative **difference** between cultures into value judgments mobilised by an **ideology** of hierarchical identification and comparison in which questions of **race** also figure extensively. As a corrective to ethnocentric tendencies, cultural relativism has stressed that cultures can not be evaluated for their merits or faults in comparison with other cultures; rather, a structural approach to ethnic cultural analysis has emerged which seeks to identify the various constituent elements and their interrelations within a culture which gives a particular culture its identity. However, such an approach is still not free from the problematic of ethnocentrism inasmuch as the act of analysis and the **epistemological** frameworks that generate analysis can still be marked invisibly by cultural assumptions.

Ethnography—Systematic and organised recording and classification of human cultures.

Existentialism—A philosophical movement that involves the study of individual existence in an infinite, unfathomable universe. Existentialism devotes particular attention to the individual's notion of free will and interpersonal responsibility without any concrete knowledge of what constitutes right and wrong. A variety of twentieth-century thinkers and writers have explored the possibilities of existentialism, including Jean-Paul Sartre, Martin Heidegger and Simone de Beauvoir, among others.

F

Facticity—The condition of being an objective fact or truth. *Facticity* is a term often used in phenomenology, as for example in a phrase such as 'the facticity of being', which suggests that although the subject always interprets the world and its phenomena, and that one only apprehends one's being in phenomenological terms, one's being has a pre-phenomenal and pre-linguistic materiality.

False consciousness—Illusory or mistaken beliefs, the term is used in marxist theories to designate the beliefs of groups with whom one disagrees or who are in need of liberation and enlightenment; otherwise, the belief on the part of the middle classes which insists that class-based interests are not positioned ideologically but are universal.

Fantasy—In everyday language, fantasy refers simply to the workings of the imagination, but in different theoretical models it has more force. In psychoanalysis, for example, fantasies are often compensatory dreams of wish-fulfilment that allow the dreamer to cope with disappointment – and the dreamer may even convince him or herself that the fantasy is real. In structuralist writings, fantasy in literature (or the fantastic) as defined by Tzvetan Todorov, refers to stories or events within them whose status is left unclear to the reader: is it real or not? The term has also been used to describe any **narrative** mode that is set in an imagined world that echoes an imagined past – especially one of dwarves and fairies (as opposed to science fiction/

cyberpunk which look to the future and to technology for fantastic effects).

Fascism—A political philosophy, movement or regime that elevates conceptions of race and nationhood over the individual. Such groups often involve a centralised, autocratic governmental structure led by a dictator. In addition to regimenting social and economic policies, fascist regimes frequently engage in the forcible suppression of their political or cultural opposition.

Fetish/ism—Sexual excitement, in Freudian discourse, brought about by the **subject**'s focus on a specific object or body part. Further employed in postcolonial discourse by Homi Bhabha in relation to the processes of racial stereotyping or in marxist discourse in relation to the mystified value of the commodity.

Fetishisation—Marxist term that refers to the manner in which mass culture **commodifies** various sociocultural concepts, ideologies or traditions.

Fiction—An imaginative story or **narrative** (including prose and verse) that offers an invented account of events.

Field—Structural term employed by Pierre Bourdieu to indicate the organisation of a given social structure determined in its meaning by identifiable social positions and their interrelations within the social sphere as these are in turn defined by the distribution and organisation of resources or **cultural capital**.

Figure—Literary term that refers to a recurring theme, image or style. As with **tropes**, figures often serve as vehicles that allow language to move beyond its literal functions and begin working in a metaphorical capacity.

Fláneur—French word defining a (mostly) male member of the monied, leisured middle classes, with the time to stroll idly and without purpose around cities and towns, observing life. Gaining popularity as a literary type in the 1890s, chiefly in Paris and associated with that other fin-de-siècle figure, the dandy, the *fláneur* enjoys the luxury of observing in an unsystematic manner the social and cultural life of the urban world, without being observed himself. German cultural critic and theorist Walter Benjamin developed the critique of the *flâneur*, principally in his *The Arcades Project*, a study of the phenomenon of urban Parisian life at the end of the nineteenth century.

Flow—Also 'flux', a term from the work of Gilles Deleuze and Félix Guattari, signifying material and **semiotic** flows (such as **desire**) which, it is argued, are not essential to human **subjectivity**, but precede the subject. Pursuing such flows, Deleuze and Guattari maintain, offers potential lines of flight and thus the **deterritorialisation** of the sovereign subject.

Foregrounding—Literary and aesthetic concept first proposed by Viktor Sklovskij, in which the artist or writer regards production as a process and not an end in itself, the purpose of which is to produce in the audience or readership a new awareness of the object or subject represented and so to understand the world differently. One means of foregrounding the process of perception and its active role in the interpretation of art is through what Sklovskij termed *ostranenie*, defamiliarisation or 'making strange', whereby the form of the art-object is revealed rather than occluded by content or subject and so how one perceives comes to be foregrounded. The artfulness involved in the production rather than the object is what is of most importance. From such a theoretical premise, it might be argued that James Joyce's *Ulysses* defamiliarises narrative convention and the assumption of realist fiction that the form of prose narrative is transparent. Foregrounding is achieved through the novelist's self-conscious techniques of drawing attention the literariness of literary language, and to the fact that language obtrudes materially between the reader and the world. Thus foregrounding effects a realisation in the reader that perception of the world is not empirical but shaped and mediated through language. The reader is always aware in a novel such as Joyce's *Ulysses* that a process is underway, in which one is expected to consider how language shapes the world and so comprehend that world and one's perception of it differently.

Form—The basic structure of a literary work of art. Form often refers to the genre of a given work, as well as to the structural interaction between the work's design and the literary content that shares in the production of its ultimate meaning.

Formalism—Refers to the critical tendency that emerged during the first half of the twentieth century and devoted its attention to concentrating on literature's formal structures in an objective manner.

Fort-Da game—In *Beyond the Pleasure Principle*, Freud recounts the observation of a game invented by his eighteen-month-old grandson. In this game the child would throw a wooden spool (to which a piece of string was attached) away from him, and then pull it back. When throwing the spool away the child would make a sound interpreted by Freud as the German *fort* (meaning 'gone away'); when pulling it back, he would say *da*, meaning 'there'. Freud interpreted the game as the child's psychic attempt to control absence and presence as a compensation for situations over which he had no control, such as his mother's temporary absences. More generally, Freud introduced through the illustration the concept of the return of the repressed.

Free indirect discourse or style—Mode of narrative presentation, which, though not directly presented as a character's speech patterns, idioms, or grammatical idiosyncrasies, presents thoughts, events or reflections as if the narrative were the character's point of view. An example of this is when James Joyce begins the story 'The Dead' with the sentence, 'Lily, the caretaker's daughter, was literally run off her feet.' Though the words are the narrator's, the figure *literally* indicates that this is what Lily thinks or what she would say. She is not literally run off her feet at all; it would be grammatically correct to say that she was figuratively run off her feet, as the phrase is a figure or idiom, obviously, for being extremely busy.

G

Gaze—Psychoanalytic concept, developed by Lacan following Jean-Paul Sartre's analysis of 'the look' and subsequently adopted in feminist and psychoanalytic film studies, which theorise the ways in which one sees another **subject** and also comprehends how one is seen. In understanding how one is looked at, the human subject comprehends that the other is also a subject. Lacan develops a theory of the gaze distinct from Sartrean conceptualisation along with the concept of *objet petit a*. In this theorisation, the gaze names the object of a scopic drive, impersonal and irreducible to the sight of the subject.

Geist—German for *spirit* or *ghost*. G.W.F. Hegel posits a theory of spirit or *geist* in his *Phenomenology of Spirit*. By this term he seeks to indicate and name a structure of reciprocal intersubjectivity. Consciousness for the self in its relation to, and comprehension of, the world is always implicitly a self-consciousness. My consciousness, in comprehending the phenomenal otherness of the objects I perceive, is always a reflective (self-)consciousness; I cannot know something without knowing that I know it. This leads to a recognition of the other being who, though distinct from oneself, is nonetheless like oneself. The other also has self-consciousness, hence the reciprocity suggested by Hegel in the intersubjective structure. Of this structure, Hegel remarks that 'a self-consciousness, in being an object, is just as much "I" as "object". With this, we already have the concept of *Spirit* . . . Spirit is . . . the absolute substance which is the unity of the different independent self-consciousnesses . . . Self-consciousness exists in and for itself, when, and by the fact that, it so exists for another, that is, it exists only in being acknowledged'. Thus *Geist* names the unity of distinct self-reflexive subjects *qua* social unity. Moreover, Hegel's thinking on *Geist* implicitly shows how the concept is fundamentally empty unless it comes into being as a result of a hermeneutics of self-conscious reciprocity. Such a determination on Hegel's part is what allows him to propose human history as a history of spirit, where spirit comes to manifest itself in and through the conscious relationships of human beings who acknowledge their shared **being**. More generally, the term denotes the manner in which we imagine or conceive of nationhood, culture and social or political movements, in the form of a shared 'spirit' which constitutes our identity as English,

German, American, Liberal, Democrat, Socialist and so on. Hence, *geist* refers to our shared assumptions – often unarticulated except as the idea of national identity, for example – or cultural **ideology,** by which sameness is asserted at the expense of that which is different or **other** within the constitution of identity. However, because the term is doubled and divided 'internally' by its different meanings and is therefore haunted by the condition of **undecidability,** there is, as Jacques Derrida argues, always something 'invisible' within the idea of *geist* which disturbs the very premise of the shared assumption which is grounded on the notion of undifferentiated identity and what that seeks to exclude but which returns nonetheless.

Gender—Term denoting the cultural constitution of notions concerning femininity or masculinity and the ways in which these serve ideologically to maintain gendered identities. In much sociological and feminist thought, gender is defined against biological sex. It represents the socially acceptable, and socially acquired, forms of being either male or female. Gender might then include everything a person does, from the clothes he or she wears, to choices of leisure activity, and from career and education to tone of voice. The concept of gender argues that a person may have male sex, but may have feminine attributes in relation to the cultural norms of his society, and vice versa, a female person may exhibit masculine traits. It provides grounds for arguing against essentialist concepts of selfhood and sex. Gender therefore describes the ways in which masculinity and femininity (the performance of gender, as opposed to the biology of sex) serve ideologically to maintain a particular status quo in society at large. More recently, the **binary opposition** underlying this kind of definition (the opposition between biology and performance) has been criticised by critics working in queer theory, particularly by Judith Butler who argues against the priority given to biology as essence that underpins even the concept that gender is performative.

Gender parody—Term often associated with Judith Butler that refers to the manner in which transvestism or drag can expose the inevitably artificial and restrictive nature of gender identity.

Genealogy—Modelled on Friedrich Nietzsche's genealogies, Michel Foucault conceives of genealogy as a method for searching for hidden structures of regulation and association, of tracing etymological, psychological and ideological ancestors of modern social, cultural or political practices. Genealogical methodology is interested in ruptures as well as continuities, contradiction as well as coherence. The genealogist, moreover, is aware of the provisional nature of her or his own **subject** position in relation to interpretations of the past, in contrast to the historian's pretence of neutrality.

Generalised communication—Term often associated with Gianni Vattimo that refers to an increasing pluralisation of groups and identities. This often media-spawned rapid proliferation results in new and disorienting social possibilities, new myths, hybrid tribes and multiple dialects and subcultures among people.

Genotext/phenotext—Corresponding terms developed in the work of Julia Kristeva referring to a set of horizontal and vertical axes establishing an organising principle structured on the functions of repetition and displacement in language. The phenotext is, for Kristeva, the conscious, structural elements of a text aiming at communication, while the genotext is the textual articulation of the unconscious, discernible in repetitive arrangements, manifestations of rhythm or tone. The genotext disrupts the ostensible 'message' or intent of a text. Put crudely, the phenotext is that part of the text that says what it says, while the genotext is that aspect governing the manner in which it communicates indirectly or, even, the manner in which it withholds communication, appears to remain silent or is otherwise fissured by gaps.

Genre—Definable types or forms of art and literature. In art, *genre painting* refers to the depiction of everyday life. In literature, while there are three genres broadly speaking – prose, poetry and drama – other more precisely genre distinctions are made, such as romance, gothic, epic, epistolary novel, science fiction, science fantasy, bildungsroman, comedy, tragedy and so on.

Globalisation—The transnational and multinational corporate tendency toward a new world order in which economic, cultural, social and political issues become increasingly driven on a global, as opposed to localised, basis.

Gothic—In the latter half of the eighteenth century and the early years of the nineteenth the term Gothic came to be associated with a literary genre, the **narratives** of which dealt with supernatural, mysterious or ghastly events and the apprehension or production of terror, and which were usually situated in wild, stormy landscapes, eerie manors or castles. Recent studies of the gothic have emphasised the role of the reader, questions of **gender**, the gothic interest in the **abject** body and corporealisation in general, and the inner feelings or phenomenological perceptions of the gothic terrain on the part of its principal protagonists. Distinctions have been made between gothic narratives of the eighteenth century, with their emphasis on mystery, and those of the nineteenth century, which explore the inner condition of the protagonist.

Grand narrative—Discourses of science, religion, politics and philosophy which are supposed to explain the world in its totality, and to produce histories of the world as **narratives** of progress. Jean-François Lyotard has, however, defined postmodernism, in part, as the collapse of such totalising explanatory frameworks.

Gynesis—Beginning with some discomfort with the term 'feminism' because the term is 'semantically tortuous and conceptually hazardous', Alice A. Jardine coins the term gynesis in order to be attentive to the methodological, political and conceptual differences within feminist thought. In particular, her concern arises out of the arguments between US and French feminisms in the early to mid 1980s. She suggests that Anglophone and Francophone feminisms have each tended to caricature the other mode of feminist practice as flawed. French feminisms were presented by the US feminist academy as both uncritically essentialist, and yet simultaneously wedded to masculist models of theoretical knowledge, especially to the writings of Marx, Lacan and Freud. American feminists on the other hand were accused by their French counterparts of wilful theoretical and political blindness in relation to the intersections that exist between sexual politics and the patriarchal bias of economics (Marx) and psychoanalytical models of human development (Lacan and Freud). Jardine's aim, therefore, was to think through the consequences of situating American experiential models of feminist activism and critical practice (what real women have politically done in the real world, what real women have experienced) within the scope of the allegedly masculist, objectivist, theoretical models then being developed in France and elsewhere in Western Europe. For Jardine, then, gynesis means 'the putting into discourse of "woman"' – placing both 'woman' and real women into the theoretical languages that have tended to exclude femininity. Her aim is thereby to permit thinkers to see in new ways. She argues that gynesis produces and reproduces neither mere representation (images of the eternal feminine, for example), nor **unmediated** reality (the experience of real women, whoever they may be). Rather, gynesis is a reading effect – a womaneffect in reading – which destabilises old versions of femininity, and undoes the **binary** of masculine ideals of femininity versus the reality of women who live in a material, not an idealised, state. It is a reading practice, and especially a creative critical practice, in which (masculine) objectivism is parodied and punctured as well as attacked on the grounds of its own illogicality (it cannot claim universality if it does not address 'woman' or women). Thus both real experience and the theoretical interventions of academic feminism conspire together in gynesis for both political (real or experiential) and academic (philosophical and theoretical) ends.

Gynocentrism—Literally, woman-centred. In critical practice, it refers to the presumption that the reader and the writer of a literary work are both female, and that the critical act is also aimed towards the woman reader.

Gynocritics—Literally, criticism of women. The term was coined by Elaine Showalter to describe a literary-critical presumption that feminist criticism would focus its attention on the works of women writers.

[H]

Habitus—Term often associated with Pierre Bourdieu referring to the mental or cognitive structures via which people interact with the larger social worlds in which they live. Bourdieu defines habitus as systems of internalised or embodied social structures that can change over time as individuals acquire new or different associations and experiences; such sets of relations and attitudes exist within what Bordieu terms a **field**. According to Bourdieu, our various forms of habitus generally find their origins in familial and educational experiences. Of particular significance to Bourdieu's conception of habitus is the notion of **cultural capital**, which individuals or social groups employ in the competitive marketplaces that characterise various aspects of social life. Bourdieu contends that social groups often cohere based upon shared systems of aesthetic taste. Bourdieu defines these 'tastes' as the 'acquired dispositions to differentiate among the various cultural objects of aesthetic enjoyment and to appreciate them differentially'. In short, habitus inspire individuals or social groups to pursue or prefer some tastes, while negating or discouraging others. Certain analysts, following Bordieu, have applied the term habitus to language, to indicate the ways in which specific social groups within a given culture define their communal identity through language use peculiar to them.

Hegemony—Term associated with Italian marxist Antonio Gramsci that refers to the cultural or intellectual domination of one school of thought, social or cultural group or **ideology** over another (or others). In defining hegemony, Gramsci relates the concept of manifestations of social coercion. This is explained through discussion of the state. For Gramsci, the state comprises political society and civil society. The dominant social group maintains its hegemonic control over subordinate or **subaltern** social groups not only through the non-coercive assertion of its cultural values and beliefs, but also through the coercive potential of its political institutions, such as education and the church.

Hermeneutic circle—The phrase is used to describe the impossibility of knowing anything except through what is already known. The phrase thus embodies a paradox: while a reader may be assumed to comprehend the entirety of a text fully only after all the component parts are understood, the various parts of the text cannot be understood until the text as a whole is discerned in its totality.

Hermeneutics—Originally a term associated with biblical exegesis and the interpretation of religious texts and especially their allegorical aspects; now more commonly employed as a defining term for a branch of interpretation developed from modern linguistics and philosophy which addresses modes of interpretation.

Herstory—Partially a pun, playing on the homophone *his story* in history, a polemical figure deployed in certain feminist critical discourses for the purpose of alerting the reader to the fact that alternative narratives and historical perspectives affirming women's point of view must be articulated.

Heterogeneity—Those elements or aspects of texts or other subjects of analysis which are dissimilar and incongruous, or which cannot be incorporated by analysis into an organic whole.

Heteroglossia—Term often associated with Mikhail Bakhtin that refers to the many discourses that occur within a given language on a microlinguistic scale; 'raznorechie' in Russian, heteroglossia literally signifies as 'different-speech-ness'. Bakhtin employed the term as a means for explaining the hybrid nature of the modern novel and its many competing utterances.

Heuristic—A heuristic argument is one that depends on assumptions garnered from past experience, or from trial and error.

History/historicism—History designates, broadly, the study or record of a series of chronological events. In addition to denoting a sphere of knowledge that explores past events, history refers to the events or phenomena that affect a given nation or institution. A somewhat vague term, historicism in critical discourse suggests either that human thought is historically grounded and undergoes **epistemological** transformations during the course of history (so that what constitutes the idea of beauty in **aesthetic** thought does not remain static but changes, for example), or that history is understood as a teleological process, whereby transformations occur as part of a general and necessary series of developments. More generally, historicism connotes an aspect of literary criticism that studies literary works within their **heterogeneous** or interrelated historical **contexts**. In addition to exploring the social or cultural forces at work in a given literary text, historical critics attempt to account for the reception and literary significance of that work in the past and the present. Historical critics recognise that literary works function as the product of the social, historical and cultural forces inherent in the era of their composition.

Homophobia—Fear and hatred of homosexuals.

Homosocial—Term coined by Eve Kosofsky Sedgwick to describe the networks of male–male relationships in literature and in culture at large. Homosociality covers a spectrum of male relationships from father and son, buddies, love rivals, sports opponents and team-mates, club members and so on – which might all be undertaken by strictly 'straight men' – through to entirely homosexual relationships at the other end of the spectrum.

Humanism/humanist—Western European philosophical discourse, the first signs of which emerged in the Early Modern Period, and, subsequently, critical mode that argues for the centrality of man (or more broadly, humanity) as a critical category; often, though not always, implicitly or explicitly secular.

Hybridity—Originally naming something or someone of mixed ancestry or derived from **heterogeneous** sources, the term has been employed in postcolonialism, particularly in the work of Homi Bhabha, to signify a reading of identities which foregrounds the work of **difference** in identity resistant to the imposition of fixed, unitary identification which is, in turn, a hierarchical location of the colonial or **subaltern subject**.

Hyperbole—A rhetorical device or figure of speech aimed at exaggeration or overstatement, the extravagance of which is not to be taken literally.

Hyperreality—Term associated with the work of Jean Baudrillard, defined succinctly by him as 'the meticulous reduplication of the real, preferably through another, reproductive medium, such as photography'. The representation of the real assumes a reality of its own, achieving a **fetishistic** condition no longer simply being the sign of the concrete real.

Hypertext—A database format in which highlighted links to other texts, databases and virtual locations are marked within a particular electronic document so as to offer further access conceptually and tangentially. Information relating to subjects are linked electronically, often through highlighted reference to a term, phrase or concept, or otherwise an author's name, important dates or the names of particular publications. In the context of literary studies and with reference to 'literary theory' in particular, George Landow has elucidated the relationships between the assumptions concerning reading, information and communication expressed by so-called poststructuralist thinkers, and the form of hypermedia in general.

Hysteria—A pathological condition involving emotional disturbance and attendant disturbance of the nervous system first defined in nineteenth-century psychology and attributed at the time mostly to women. Hysterics were usually considered to have enfeebled emotional, intellectual or moral capabilities.

$\boxed{\text{I}}$

Icon—Identified in modern **semiotics** as a particular type of sign wherein there is a resemblance, rather than an arbitrary relationship, between the **signifier** and **signified**.

Id—That part of the unconscious in psychoanalytic theory comprising instinctive, and therefore pre-rational, impulses.

Idealism—Belief in a transcendent or metaphysical truth beyond reality.

Identity politics—Refers to the ideologies of **difference** that characterise politically motivated movements and schools of literary criticism such as multiculturalism, in which diversity or ethnicity functions as the principal issue of political debate.

Ideological state apparatus—Term coined by Louis Althusser. Althusser argues that ideology is not only a matter of ideas or mechanisms of representation but of material practices which exist in the form of apparatuses and institutions, such as schools, the church and so on. Literature is not simply a text but a production of legal, educational and cultural institutions.

Ideology—Broadly defined, a system of cultural assumptions, or the discursive concatenation of beliefs or values which uphold or oppose social order, or which otherwise provide a coherent structure of thought that hides or silences the contradictory elements in social and economic formations. However, despite the apparent straightforwardness of this outline just provided, ideology is a notoriously difficult and equivocal concept to define. Part of ideology's slipperiness comes from its own strategic ability to serve in the definition of other concepts in equivocal, if not **ambivalent** and even antagonistic or **dialectical** ways. Its modern uses within literary and cultural studies have tended to have developed from and been influenced by marxist and post-marxist thinking, even while, within marxian discourse, there is still debate and contention over a word and concept which is notable for its absence from Marx's *Das Kapital*. While definitions vary to greater or lesser degrees in their understanding of the definition and application of ideology, as well as the **contexts** defining the use of the term, what can be said is that ideology always bears on material conditions of lived existence. Briefly however, and to return to the beginning of this definition, ideology may be defined as that nexus of beliefs or ideas which, formed as more or less a dominant consensus at any particular historical moment and as the discursive, philosophical and imaginary mediation of lived social, political, economic and cultural relations, serves to perpetuate or otherwise is put to work in the maintenance of social and civil relationships.

Terry Eagleton has defined ideology succinctly as those 'ideas and beliefs which help to legitimate the interests of a ruling group or class specifically by distortion and dissimulation'. Noting the tendentious nature of definitions pertaining to ideology, Raymond Williams has suggested that three principal definitions may be offered. These are, in Williams' words: 'a system of beliefs characteristic of a particular class or group . . . a system of illusory beliefs – false ideas or false consciousness – which can be contrasted with true or scientific knowledge . . . [and] the general process of the production of meanings and ideas'.

Such definitions resonate with that provided by Louis Althusser, who states that 'ideology is the system of ideas and representations which dominate the mind of a man or a social group . . . Ideology represents the imaginary relationship of individuals to their real conditions of existence'. Althusser offers a systematic definition of ideology, which structural model is in part anticipated in the work of Antonio Gramsci (see **hegemony**), through an investigation of the ways in which social and cultural forces most economically perpetuate and reproduce the conditions by which capitalist modes of production continue. Within the **capitalist** state, for example, education serves the interests of the ruling classes by attempting to instill competence, attentiveness and submission to the rules favoured by the dominant social order. Similarly religion, via its institutional manifestation in the church, teaches moral values appropriate to and approved by the ruling order. Thus education and the church belong to what Althusser terms 'ideological state apparatuses'. Ideology is thus coercive in the workings of its power, and is shown by Althusser to unite various institutions of the state.

The idea of ideology remains though notoriously contested, and its very slipperiness seems to indicate its power. Slavoj Žižek has acknowledged the ways in which ideology appears to signify a broad spectrum of attitudes and beliefs, if not a medium by which human subjectivity is **interpellated**. In attesting to such slippage and resistance to definition, Žižek draws our attention to the essentially 'psychic' or imaginary nature of ideology, as though society, before and beyond the individual subject, had something akin to an '**unconscious**'. Yet, in implying such a comprehension, Žižek rejects the notion of ideology as simply illusion or false consciousness. The subject's interpellation within capitalist society is ideological but has material effects and consequences.

Illocutionary speech act—(see **constative speech act**).

Imaginary/Symbolic/Real—Jacques Lacan's version of psychoanalytic thought posits three psychic realms. The aim of the 'healthy' adult is to achieve a certain mastery within the Symbolic realm: that is, the realm of ordered, structured paraphrasable language, the realm of Law. However, the Symbolic realm is not ideal because language itself is, following Saussure, conventional, and only arbitrarily connected to the objects it describes. Indeed, language in Lacan's definition describes what is not there. He argues that a child learns to speak in response to the absence of his object of **desire** (the mother, or her breast); he learns to say 'I want' and thus becomes initiated into the beginnings of his necessary if painful accommodation with the Symbolic. This process of 'joining' the Symbolic order begins with the **mirror phase** which initiates the child into the beginnings of language after he catches sight of himself – or rather of a reflection of himself – in a mirror, and recognises himself for the first time as a separate and distinct **being**, not one with either the world or with his mother. Lacan calls this very early beginning of acculturation 'Imaginary' because the mirror image that reveals the child to himself is, in fact, merely an image – or a signifier. His recognition of himself is therefore a misrecognition of an image, not a fact. No one, Lacan argues, no matter how well adjusted, ever leaves the Imaginary realm completely; there are always Imaginary residues (misrecognitions) even in the most powerful Symbolic forms. The Real, Lacan's third realm, is by far the least important. He uses the term to refer to the merely contingent accidents of everyday life that impinge on our **subjectivity**, but which have no fundamental psychic causes or meanings: trapping your hand in the car door might hurt, but it doesn't signify, and it belongs to the realm of the Real.

Imago—Psychoanalytic term for a subjective image of an authority figure, such as a parent, which influences behaviour and attitudes.

Imperialism—Refers to the systematic policies of territorial expansion by which one culture or nation appropriates the land, people and resources of another to further its **colonial** ends; also, the practices and discourses which promote and maintain the cultural, economic and **ideological** assumptions underpinning the dominance of one nation by another. In *Culture and Imperialism*, Edward Said argues that imperialism names the practices, attitudes, and theories 'of a dominating metropolitan centre ruling a distant territory', and that colonialism, defined by Said as the occupation of that territory, is the consequence of imperialism.

Implicature—Term coined in 1975 by speech-act philosopher H. P. Grice and subsequently employed within discourse analysis. Implicature refers to the inherent indirection in spoken discourse. Grice contends that we use such statements as means for sharing a series of what he describes as 'communicative presumptions'.

Implied author—Term associated with Wayne Booth, who distinguishes between the *real* and *implied* author. The latter is an idealised figure, distinct from the narrator. The implied author, defined by Booth as the 'core of norms and choices' which dominate a given text, is discernible through the reader's assumptions about the moral, political and other values which are expressed by the text as a whole, regardless of the real author's statements on such matters outside the text (in interviews and so forth). The three formal aspects of a text which serve to define the implied author are *style, tone* and *technique*.

Implied reader—Wolfgang Iser defines the *implied reader* as a hypothetical figure or concept produced through the assumptions, beliefs, historical knowledge, and philosophical and political positions embedded in and constituting the structure of a given text.

Intentional fallacy—Term coined by W. K. Wimsatt and Monroe C. Beardsley to describe critical methods that seek to interpret a literary work by reference to the **author's intentions**. Wimsatt and Beardsley argued that this position was necessarily untenable since (a) the author's intentions could never be satisfactorily recovered; and (b) the work could only be read and judged in its own terms, without reference to extra-textual information.

Interpellation—Marxist term often associated with the work of Louis Althusser denoting the ways in which subjects within an ideological system are placed in false positions of knowledge regarding themselves or otherwise constituted by an illusory self-knowledge the premise of which is autonomy; the subject, in comprehending him- or herself as having agency or freedom is positioned and placed in a self-deluding location with regard to his or her autonomy by external forces serving dominant capitalist interests. As Slavoj Žižek describes interpellation, 'when the subject recognises himself in an ideological call, he automatically overlooks the fact that this very formal act of recognition creates the content one recognises oneself in'. The subject thus engages in a symbolic and ideological (self-)identification which is at the same time a fundamental misrecognition of his or her subjectivity constituted within social, material reality.

Interpretive community—Concept developed in reader response theory by Stanley Fish. Fish proposes that a reader's interpretation of a text is governed by the interpretive community or communities that govern the cultural assumptions about how one reads, meaning, interpretation, value and so on. For Fish, one is never outside one's interpretive community because one cannot define the limits of any presumed community as such; moreover, the impossibility of assigning limits to an interpretive community is impossible because such communities, in communicating with one another, are porous and malleable.

Intersubjectivity—Denotes the concept of intercommunication between separate, conscious minds. Intersubjectivity also connotes the capacity for becoming accessible to multiple subjects.

Intertextuality—Term coined originally by Julia Kristeva, intertextuality refers to the ways in which all utterances (whether written or spoken) necessarily refer to other utterances, since words and linguistic/grammatical structures pre-exist the individual speaker and the individual speech. Intertextuality can take place consciously, as when a writer sets out to quote from or allude to the works of another. But it always, in some sense, takes place in all utterance.

Intervention—Term often associated with theorist Gayatri Chakravorty Spivak that refers to the political act or strategy of entering into, or 'intervening' in, a given debate or historical moment so as to have a voice on a particular subject.

Introjection—Term employed in psychoanalysis by Sandor Ferenczi to indicate the formation of a subjective mental image of an external object. In the process of introjection, the subject internalises the emotional tie that he or she has formed with the object, and transfers the psychic energy previously directed toward the object of desire to the image as a substitute for a libidinal connection.

Irony—The contradiction, incongruity or discrepancy between appearance or expectation and reality. Irony can be understood in terms of events, situations, and the structural components of literature. Dramatic irony involves a situation in which a given character's statements come back to haunt him or her, while tragic irony refers to situations in which the protagonist's tragic end is foreshadowed by a sense of foreboding and misinformation. Structural irony reflects a given author's attempt to establish an ironic layer of meaning throughout a text, often by virtue of the ironic distance provided by the narration of a literary work.

Isotopy—A semantic strategy that allows for a uniform reading of a story.

Iterability/iteration—Idea, formalised in the work of Jacques Derrida, specifically in *Limited Inc*, which, as a quasi-concept, challenges the very idea of the stability of concepts and conceptuality in general. Iterability does not signify repetition simply; it signifies an alterability within the repetition of the same: a novel is a novel, generically, but every novel will inevitably differ from every other. Thus the concept of the novel is destabilised by our experience of every novel we read and, argues Derrida, we have to deal with the paradox of the simultaneity of sameness *and* **difference**.

[J]

Jouissance—Literally, in French, 'pleasure, enjoyment' but with legal connotations relating to property and rights, lost in translation, referring to the right to enjoy. The word has come to be used in psychoanalytic and feminist theories to mean more especially pleasures associated with sensuous and sexual gratification, or orgasm. As such, it refers to a fulfilment that is necessarily merely temporary, and that must therefore always be sought anew.

[K]

Kenosis—Greek term for 'emptying', traditionally employed within Christian Theology referring the idea of Christ's renunciation of the power of incarnation. Harold Bloom employs the term in *The Anxiety of Influence* to suggest the revisionary process by which a poet 'empties' or 'isolates' himself from his or her poetic influences so as to create a poetry which is not simply a repetition of the precursor's influence in other words. The term is also associated with the work of Gianni Vattimo which refers, particularly in feminist theology, to the notion of 'self-emptying', or giving oneself to the world.

Kitsch—Sentimental, vulgar and pretentious or melodramatic art, which because of these attributes is considered aesthetically deficient. The term originally appeared in use in the 1860s and 1870s, in the art markets of Munich, where it came to signify highly popular and saleable art or reproductions popular with the bourgeoisie. In the twentieth century, modes of representation based on kitsch values began to be appropriated by avant-garde artists in order to foreground, and thereby estrange and question the work of art and its aesthetic role in high culture. Kitsch calls into question the supposedly existent boundaries between works of high culture and popular culture. Jeff Koons is amongst the most recent artists to work with kitsch and related modes of art that challenge aesthetic sensibility and preconceived notions of art. One aspect of Koons' work is to make high quality porcelain reproductions of everyday objects. In popular culture, garden gnomes might be considered kitsch, as would oil paintings on velvet.

L

Labour theory of value—Tendency of the value (or price) of goods produced and sold under competitive conditions to be in proportion to the labour costs incurred during production.

Language—Refers to words, their pronunciation and their syntactical combination in order to be understood by a community. Language similarly denotes a given system for communicating ideas or feelings via the use of signs, sounds, gestures or marks.

Langue/parole—In Saussurean linguistics, *langue* refers to the whole system of a given language (its grammar, vocabulary and syntax); *parole* refers to the individual instance of utterance that takes place under the framework of the *langue*. Saussure's interest was primarily in the study of the system or *langue*.

Latent/manifest content—Psychoanalytic, specifically Freudian terms relating to dream imagery and the unconscious. *Latent content* refers to the traces, signs and images embedded inaccessibly in the unconscious. When these pass, as it were, into the dream, they become translated into the images, events and symbols that one remembers as making up the dream. Such transformed images and the narrative they compose are the *manifest content*.

Liberal humanism—Often used as a pejorative term, the values of liberal humanism have to do with democracy, decency, tolerance, rationality, the belief in human progress and a whole-hearted support of the individual against the machinations of 'inhuman' political systems. The problem of liberal humanism is that it frequently lapses into **universalism** or **idealism,** and has no proper responses to totalitarianism where the individual is frankly powerless. It is a belief system that also disguises the very profound inequities and horrors of even Western democratic societies. It is a rejection of systematised thought in return for a generalised belief in the essential goodness of most people most of the time.

Libidinal economy— By positing the libidinal as an 'economy', Jean-François Lyotard reads **desire** as a material, rather than simply psychic, process. He is less concerned with what desire 'is' than in how it functions. He sees desire as the energy of society, but an unstable energy, unpredictably connecting the psychological to the economical in a type of feeling and desire Lyotard calls an 'intensity'. **Narrative**, broadly defined as a poem or an advertisement, binds these moments of intensities into an apparently coherent pattern in order to exploit the power residing there.

Libido—In psychoanalytic discourse and theory, a psychic energy or drive associated with sexual instinct.

Life-world—Philosophical concept, originally German (*lebenswelt*), signifying all the experiences, events and interactions of a particular life.

Liminality—From the Latin, *limen*, meaning threshold, liminality signifies a condition of being at a threshold or limit, spatially or temporally. Textual analysis of liminality draws attention to the passage across limits, boundaries or thresholds in **narratives**, where the limit being crossed is constituted as an assemblage of culturally significant values.

Lipogram—An experimental piece of writing or literary game from which are excluded all words containing particular letters, or a single letter. As constraint and game, writing a lipogram forces the writer to be inventive in a number of different ways. Edgar Allen Poe's *The Raven* was written as a conscious lipogram, in that the author decided to omit the letter *z* from the writing. This is however relatively easy in comparison with the avoidance of the vowels, and other more common consonants. Perhaps the most well-known example of such writing is Georges Perec's novel *A Void*, in which Perec imposes the constraint on writing the novel of omitting any words spelt with an *e*, the most common letter in both English words and French, Perec's own language. Gilbert Adair's translation of the novel similarly avoids the letter *e*.

Lisible/scriptible—Used by Roland Barthes in the definition of types of text, the terms are translatable as 'readable' and 'writerly' respectively. The readerly text does all the work for the reader, leaving the reader the role of passive consumer. The writerly text makes the reader work and resists the conventions of readerly or realist textuality, principally the assumptions of linguistic transparency and the self-evidence of meaning.

Literature—At its most neutral, and broadest, *literature* signifies textual manifestations of **writing**. The term also refers to the production of literary works and to specific bodies of poetry or prose. *Literature* has been used to designate any 'imaginative', 'creative' or 'fictional' writing, whether in poetry, drama or prose. There is, furthermore, in the use of the term an implicit **aesthetic** or other form of **value** judgement, so that some works are considered literary while others are not. Another determination of *literature* is in a recognition of the use of language in particular ways which transform so-called ordinary or everyday speech, through **tropological** estrangement or intensification, for example. One perspective is that literary language, or certain aspects of it and the way in which it functions, is noticeable in that it draws attention to its departures from everyday utterances. Another perspective is that **context** can determine the definition of literature, whether this is a matter of institutional **authority** or a marketing device which announces a book as a 'novel'. The question of the literary therefore comes down not necessarily to any perceivable intrinsic qualities as it does to acts of **reading** and the ways in which reading directs itself to particular aspects of a text rather than others.

Litotes—From the Greek meaning *small, plain, meagre*, a figure of speech in which an idea is conveyed through the expression of a negated antonym, such as 'the argument is not unsuccessful'.

Locutionary speech act—(see **constative speech act**).

Logocentrism—Term ascribed to Jacques Derrida that refers to the nature of Western thought, language and culture since Plato's era. The Greek signifier for 'word,' 'speech' and 'reason', logos possesses connotations in Western culture for law and truth. Hence, logocentrism refers to a culture that revolves around a central set of universal principles or beliefs. More specifically, logocentrism denominates that process in the history of Western thought which, since Aristotle, privileges speech over **writing** as being closer to mental experience. Thus, for Derrida the history of metaphysics in the West is the history of logocentrism. The logocentric insistence in Western philosophy on the priority of voice over writing belongs to a metaphysics of presence.

M

Machine subjectivity—Term associated with Félix Guattari that refers to 'semiotic productions of the mass media, of computers, of telecommunications, robotics, etc., outside of psychological subjectivity'. For Guattari, the technologies of information and communication serve to reorient and transform the thinking of subjectivity in terms of **heterogeneous** semiotic flows. Machinic subjectivity is productive, 'polyphonic' and irreducibly multiform rather than unifying. However, while it may be productive in hitherto undreamt of ways, Guattari warns that machine subjectivity has the potential for a 'mind-numbing mass mediatization'.

Manicheanism—Belief in a kind of philosophical or religious dualism.

Masculinity/femininity—Binary opposition which refers to the construction of attributes of identity associated with or based on a given individual's **sexuality** or **gender**-ascribed perspectives and/or culturally encoded value systems concerning behaviour.

Masquerade—In contemporary gender theory, the concept of masquerade, derived from the writings of Joan Rivière, is central, particularly her essay 'Womanliness as a Masquerade' (1929). It argues that gender is a performance rather than a natural phenomenon with which one is born; it has to be acquired, learned and polished and is in no sense natural.

Mass culture—Term often associated with British cultural theorist Richard Hoggart that refers to a new commercialised social order that finds its roots in the mass dissemination of television, radio, magazines and a variety of other media; in

Hoggart's view, mass culture shapes and reconstructs cultural, social, and intellectual life in its image and via its **mediated** depiction of artificial levels of reality.

Master/slave dialectic—Hegel's model for understanding the interaction between two self-consciousnesses and the manner in which each entity considers the **other** in terms of the **self**. Hegel argues that this admittedly 'primitive' model reveals the ways in which each figure functions as a 'mirror' for the **other** and ultimately eschews co-operation because of their inherently subordinate relationship.

Materialism—Doctrine or system of beliefs that maintains that economic or social change occurs via material well-being rather than intellectual or spiritual phenomena.

Mediation—Concept of textual transformation, often employed in marxist and other materialist criticisms, which supersedes reductive or crude models of **reflection** which assume either that the economic **base** is reflected in its cultural superstructure or that any given text simply reflects the world, instead of mediating that image and thereby shaping or influencing the reader's comprehension in a particular way. Also, the notion of mediation is employed to suggest that the text is itself not a simple recording or representation but is influenced in its shaping by a number of factors including matters of historical, cultural and **ideological** relation.

Metacriticism—Critical mode which takes the act of criticism, its principles, processes, concerns and interests, as its principal subject. Works such as Terry Eagleton's *Literary Theory: An Introduction* or Jonathan Culler's *Structuralist Poetics* are, typically, works definable as metacritical.

Metafiction—A fictional mode that takes fictionality – the conventions of writing fiction – as part of its own subject matter.

Metahistory—Analysis of principles governing historical narrative or the structures of such narrative.

Metalanguage—Roman Jakobson defines metalanguage as any form of language which defines linguistic properties. Following the work of Alfred Tarski, Colin MacCabe describes metalanguage which announces its object languages as material, and signals them so through the conventions of the imposition of quotation marks and other diacritical markers, while assuming an implicit transparency for itself. Thus, for MacCabe, the 'narrator' or '**narrative** voice' in a realist novel assumes the role of a metalanguage, in that it appears to 'observe' rather than to interpret or analyse.

Metalepsis—Substitution of one metonym with another, or more generally, any series of successive figurative supplements.

Metaphor—A figure of speech in which two unlike objects are situated in comparison to one another. While some metaphors perform decorative functions, metaphors often serve as functional or structural means of comparison. Metaphors involving vastly unrelated elements are referred to as mixed metaphors.

Metaphysics—Originally derived from the order of Aristotle's works, where all writings that did not fit within the various disciplines were put together in a volume 'next to the physics', metaphysics has come to mean the total structure of a philosophical system trying to determine **being** as such and in general. Accordingly metaphysical systems differ according to the relation they posit between **ontology** (the philosophy of being), **epistemology**, **ethics** and politics. At the same time metaphysics characterises a thinking that determines the physical by means of a principle that resides outside of this world, such as God, for example. One distinguishes between a *metaphysica specialis*, concerning questions for the divine being, immortality and freedom, and a *metaphysica generalis*, determining the meaning of being as such and in general.

Metonymy—A figure of speech in which one object or idea is substituted for another, related object or idea in order to produce an aesthetic or literary effect.

Mimesis—Can be used in two distinct ways. First, mimesis (from the Greek *mimos*, a mime) refers to the imitation or representation of reality in art. Mimesis can also be used to describe the process by which one writing mimics another kind: for example, a fiction might pretend to be a historical document in order to gain **authority** for its account.

Mimicry—Generally, the practice, act or art of imitation, often for the purpose of ridicule. Homi Bhabha uses the term to identify a form of colonial control of its **subjects**. The coloniser seeks to impose on the colonial subject the forms and values of the colonial master, so the Anglicisation of Indians and Africans during British colonial rule. However, as Bhabha identifies, there remains a gap between the desire to erase **difference**, indicated by Bhabha in the phrase 'not white/not quite', from which emerges **ambivalence**.

Mirror phase—Jacques Lacan posited that a baby, at first an oceanic bundle of undifferentiated **desire** who believes himself to be continuous with the larger world and his mother, first comes to a realisation of himself as a unitary and separate **being** when, at age 6–18 months, he first sees his own reflection in a mirror. For Lacan, this is the beginning of the **ego's** development, but it is significantly founded on a misapprehension, since the image in the mirror is a signified – a substitute image of the **self**, not the self itself. Hence, the mirror phase implies that the ego is founded on highly unstable grounds rather than in any essential personality.

Mise en abyme—From the French for 'placed into the abyss', mise en abyme has come to mean **narrative** or philosophical moments of infinite regression. Although Chinese boxes or other infinite regressive features are often used for comic effect, the French term emphasises the terror of emptiness that is also part of the free play of language where language has only the most tangential, arbitrary and conventionalised relationships with reality.

Mnemotechnic—Literally, the work of memory or that which memory causes to appear. The concept of mnemotechnic combines the idea of involuntary memory, the idea that memory is not passively stored in the mind but is, instead, an active force which can return without conscious effort, with that of impersonal memory through the effects of chance association and signification. Thus a literary text may be said to be produced out of, while actively producing, preserving and remembering personal, social and cultural pasts beyond the immediate **intentions of the author**.

Mode of production—Marxist concept in the theory of historical materialism that accounts for the historical conditions by which productive forces such as labour, the work force, technology, materials, and tools combine in particular, historically determined ways with distribution of wealth, social power structures, ownership and control of power relations in society, the law, and class-relations to form an organic totality, which maintains and sustains social and economic order.

Modernism—Term referring to the literary, artistic and general culture of the first half of the twentieth century. Modernism is distinguished by its general rejection of previous literary traditions, particularly those of the late nineteenth century and of **bourgeois** society. In addition to involving an existentialist view of the universe, modernists explore myth as a device of formal organisation.

Modernity—From one perspective, modernity may be defined as the condition of embracing or reflecting the value systems inherent in modernism's intellectual value systems, as 'modernism' signifies a project identifiable with intellectual and artistic projects of the early twentieth century. However, the idea of modernity is a vexed one, not least because there is little agreement as to where the moment of modernity, whether in **epistemological** terms or in terms of modes of production and social and economic relations, emerges historically. There are arguments that initial instances of modernity or 'early' modernity are coterminous with the development of notions of **subjectivity**, corporeality and autonomy in the Renaissance or, as it is alternatively described, the Early Modern Period typified by the emergence of humanist thought. On the other hand, modernity is also identified as a specifically 'Enlightenment' project, related in particular to the thinking of the inevitability of progress. At the same time, the emergence of modernity has been assigned to the transition between feudal social formations and the emergence of the nation state, the beginning of colonial enterprise and nascent manifestations of pre-capitalist modes of production. Whichever cultural, intellectual and historical set of circumstances one identifies with or as the idea of the modern, what is consistent in these arguments is the idea that modernity emerges as a struggle, critical tension or even break with its forebears. At the same time, it is argued that that which is comprehended as modern, while opening a gap between its own instance and the past, still bears traces of that past in its own thinking. Another aspect of the conceptualisation of modernity, drawn chiefly from the work of Martin Heidegger and Walter Benjamin, is a transformation in the relationships between society and technology, relationships which are examined extensively in the work of, for example, Paul Virilio, Giorgio Agamben and Gianni Vattimo.

Molar/molecular—Terms employed in the work of Gilles Deleuze and Félix Guattari, to describe the processes constituting the organisation of the human **subject**. The Molar signifies the territorially defined stability of conscious awareness (see **deterritorialisation**). The molecular are those unconscious elements in their multiplicities which constitute the **flows** of **desiring machines**, which are brought to a halt, and thereby stabilised, or otherwise excluded within the molar organisation of **consciousness**. It is the function of **schizoanalysis** to destabilise and **deterritorialise** the flows and their molar organisation, so as to accommodate without limiting the processes of molecular **becoming**.

Monist—A person who reduces all phenomena to a single viewpoint or principle; also, a given individual who views reality as the product of a singular, unified vision, rather than as the sum of a series of component parts. Monist analysis that focuses solely or primarily on one form of domination (for example, gender, race or class).

Monologism—Term coined by Mikhail Bakhtin to describe characters representing multiple points of view while being clearly dominated by a single voice or **ideology**.

Morpheme—The smallest linguistic or structural unit of language.

Multiculturalism—Refers to the social and political movement and/or position that views **differences** between individuals and groups to be a potential venue of cultural strength and renewal; multiculturalism celebrates and explores different varieties of experience stemming from racial, ethnic, gender, sexual and/or class differences.

Multiplicative analysis—Analysis developed by feminists of colour. It seeks to account for the experiences of people who have been subordinated to several forms of domination. Whereas an additive approach would see (for example) race, class and gender as three discrete systems that accumulate oppressions on poor women of colour, a multiplicative approach analyses how race and class change the meanings of gender, how race and gender change the meanings of class, and how class and gender change the meanings of race. A multiplicative approach highlights the differential experiences of women of colour rather than their 'double' or 'triple' oppression. Finally, a multiplicative approach is contextual and historically informed. It recognises that in certain cases, one of the features (race, gender, class, sexuality, etc.) may be more salient than the others. Also called multiaxial analysis, or intersectionality.

Myth—The traditional story of pseudo-historical events that functions as a fundamental element within the worldview of a given people or nation. Myths are similarly employed by human communities to attempt to explain the nature of various practices, beliefs or natural phenomena.

Mytheme—Neologism coined by Claude Lévi-Strauss to indicate the structural elements or units that recur in different narrative, mythological structures, based on his understanding of the analogical similarity between the structural forms of linguistics and myth.

$\boxed{\text{N}}$

Name of the father (*Le nom du père*)—Phrase used by Jacques Lacan in relation to the Oedipus complex, which signals the **subject's** comprehension of paternal or authoritative prohibition, a prohibition constitutive of **authority**. Lacan plays on the homophonic quality of the French for name (*nom*), which sounds like the French for 'no' (*non*).

Narratee—The person to whom a narrative is directed, whether a character or characters in a narrative, such as those to whom Marlow tells of his journey down the Congo in Conrad's *Heart of Darkness*, or the real or implied reader of any narrative.

Narrative—At its most fundamental, a narrative is an account of events, whether real or fictional. However, narrative differs from the idea of a simple unordered account or report of events (supposing such a thing to be possible). Gérard Genette offers a sustained account of narrative structure and form in his *Narrative Discourse*, which addresses five principal aspects of narrative: (a) order of events; (b) duration of events and the time it takes to tell incidents; (c) frequency or repetition of events and how such recurrences shape the narrative form from the basic **diegesis**; (d) mood, by which Genette indicates the narrator's point of view, perspective, distance or proximity to the events narrated; (e) narrative voice. For Genette, the analysis of narrative concerns itself and implies the study of a series of relationships which make up narrative, these being (a) the relationship between a particular discourse and the events which are retold through that discourse, and (b) the relationship between the discourse and the act of narration. Thus there is for Genette a tripartite structure at its most basic to any narrative: discourse, narration, event, or, as he formulates it, analysis of narrative is 'a study of the relationships between narrative and story, between narrative and narrating, and . . . story and narrating'. Studying narrative is therefore not simply comprehending it as an account but also an analytical understanding of how a narrative is given the shape it has, why certain events have greater significance than others in relation to the totality of the narrative, and how events retold are shaped by the act of narration or the role of the narrator.

Narratology—Theory and systematic study of **narrative**, and especially the study of the structural, formal and temporal elements of narrative and the relationships between them. Narratology will address the functions of duration, repetition, the chronological or anachronic reordering of events out of a progressive temporal linear sequence, the role of the narrator and the various levels of discourse, along with their hierarchical or **architectonic** relationships, which constitute narrative structure.

Negritude—Neologism to define the political, cultural and historical affirmation and consciousness of Black culture of collective African heritage and origin, conceived by poet Aimé Césaire in the 1930s.

Neoimperialism—Relating to the manner in which nations, policies or practices extend their dominion or **authority** over other, often less economically or culturally viable others.

Neurosis—In psychology, a disabling or distressing disorder, often manifesting itself in irrational anxiety.

Nihilism—Philosophical rejection of all systems of belief, whether religious or secular, and a denial of the meaning of moral systems. Also a term applied to the existential despair in the face of a presumed lack of meaning or purpose to life. Also, nihilism is interpreted as a destructive or negative, hostile attitude towards institutions and structures of belief.

Nomad/ism/nomadology—Term associated with the work of Gilles Deleuze and Félix Guattari which figurally stresses the possibility of thinking differently, and which is given extended consideration in their *A Thousand Plateaus*. Deleuze and Guattari's concern in employing this term is not with a particular content of thought so much as with the utopian expression of an other modality of thought beyond dominant philosophical models. Deleuze does not propose an absolute model of nomadic thinking but merely suggests, idealistically and as a hope, its possibility. Nomadic thinking would be *just* thinking which does not remain within epistemological territories. Indeed, a feature of nomadism in thought would be its **flow** and, with that, its **deterritorialisation** of structured models or disciplines of thought. Concomitant on that flow of nomadic thinking would be its strategic 'weakness', that is to say the abandonment of the aggressiveness typical of territorial modes of thought. Furthermore, nomadic thinking *is* nomadic – it drifts, often from itself, in that it is not centred on any authoritative, governing or originary principal by which it might ground itself (and thereby defend its 'territory') and to which it might return.

Nominalism—A theory that argues against the notion of universal essences in reality and maintains that only individual perspectives, rather than abstract generalities, exist.

Normativity—The postulation of **hegemonic**, culturally prescribed norms or standards such as heterosexuality.

Nouveau roman—French term that translates as 'new novel', referring to a movement that developed in the 1950s and continued in the 1960s. Its practitioners included Phillipe Sollers, Nathalie Sarraute, Alain Robbe-Grillet, Marguerite Duras and Claude Simon. In the *nouveau roman* many of the conventions of realism and other traditional novel forms were abandoned in favour of more experimental narrative modes in order to convey more accurately the random and discontinuous nature of modern experience.

[O]

Objectification—The manner in which various individuals or social groups treat others as objects and expressions of their own senses of reality; reducing an **other**'s sense of **being** into a form that can be experienced universally by other individuals and social groups.

Objective correlative—Concept defined by T. S. Eliot, to indicate the expression of emotion through aesthetic form. Eliot suggests that an emotion is produced in the reader through a particular patterning of 'a set of objects, a situation, [or] a chain of events which shall be the formula of that *particular* emotion'.

Objet petit a—A complex term from Lacanian psychoanalysis. Lacan suggested that objects of **desire** are always changing because the desiring **subject** is always changing too. He wanted to find a term to describe the mutability and mortality of the desired object, and to describe it in a way that disrupted what he saw as the stability of the **binary** 'desiring subject/desired object' in Freudian thought. The term he came up with is 'objet petit a', where 'a' stands for 'autre' (French for **other**), distinguished from the Other elsewhere in his writing by the lower case initial letter. Objet petit a can be anything at all that is touched by desire. Desire is fleeting and mutable hence the object of desire is always in flux and is always just out of reach or just beyond the field of vision. In many ways, then, the term stands for desire, always understood by Lacan as absent and unattainable, but always equally constitutive of the subject (who is what he or she desires or lacks).

Oedipus complex—In Freudian psychoanalysis the Oedipus complex refers to the whole complex of both loving and hostile feeling experienced by a child towards its parents in the process of achieving acculturated maturity. The Oedipus complex manifests itself as an intense rivalry, including the horrifying wish for his or her death, with the parent of the same sex for the love of the parent of the opposite sex (which is to be understood as a libidinal or sexualised desire). Negotiation of this complex, the relinquishing of forbidden (incestuous) desire and its **displacement** onto suitable substitute objects (a boy must love not his mother, but a woman *like* his mother; a girl must love not her father, but a baby given to her by a man *like* her father) is required to achieve healthy adulthood. The complex is never completely successfully negotiated, however, and there are always residual Oedipal problems in even the healthiest of adults.

Ontic—Relating to epistemological enquiry concerning the real rather than the phenomenal **being**, existence or structure of entities.

Ontology—Branch of philosophy addressing the meaning or essence of **being**.

Ontotheology—Any form of **ontological** or, in general, metaphysical determination, modelled on theology, in terms of a uniquely superior **being**, concept or word, such as the divine of theology.

Orientalism—Term coined by Edward Said naming the ensemble of Western, usually though not exclusively European discourses and other forms of representation of non-Western cultures. Said traces the history of Orientalist discourses in literature, the arts and other documents from the eighteenth century onwards.

Other/otherness—Term employed throughout critical discourse in differing ways, otherness names the quality or state of existence of **being** other or different from established norms and social groups; the distinction that one makes between one's self and others, particularly in terms of sexual, ethnic and relational senses of **difference**; in Lacanian psychoanalysis, there is the other and the Other: the former signifies that which is not really other but is a reflection and projection of the **ego**; the latter signifies a radical **alterity** irreducible to any imaginary or subjective identification. In the texts of Luce Irigaray, the other indicates the position always occupied by woman within patriarchal culture and other masculinist cultures which privileges masculinity as self-sameness, or otherwise a signifier of presence, origin or centrality.

Overdetermination—The act or practice of overemphasising, or resolving in an excessive fashion, a given conclusion or psychological factor. Alternatively, a text which is said to be overdetermined is available for multiple readings from various, **heterogeneous**, if not theoretically or polemically incompatible positions. The term has its most specific theoretical uses in the psychoanalytical and marxist praxes of, respectively, Sigmund Freud and Louis Althusser. For Freud, the psyche produces representations, significations and meanings in situating the **subject** in relation to his or her world. However, how we produce meaning is not entirely (if at all) within our conscious control because the **unconscious** determines meaning through its generation and juxtaposition of images and symbols. Thus, the human mind generates overdetermined meaning where images and representations signify in more than a single manner. Meanings are produced in excess of the psyche's capability to comprehend, control or organise at any one time. For example, any dream is the result of the symbolic construction which is produced by the unconscious, but every signifying element, every image, sign or representation, verbal or visual, is overdetermined by the work of the unconscious, inasmuch as its meaning is always multiple and therefore available to different interpretations or analyses.

Within certain strands of marxism, the notion of over-determination, which Althusser imports specifically from Freud, operates at a social and cultural, rather than an individual, level. Overdetermination is closely related to the concept of contradiction, originating in G.W.F. Hegel's writings, and first given an explicitly marxist articulation in a 1937 essay by Mao Zedong. Mao formulates the historical situation of China in the 1930s through an examination, as Arif Dirlik has put it, 'of the contradictoriness of its various moments [such as the contradiction between national and social needs], and the articulation of this contradictoriness as a contradiction between theory and practice'. The contradictory elements of society at a given historical moment produce an overdetermined identity for that society, Mao argues, and, as a result of this, social contradiction is, 'the basic law of **materialist dialectics**'. Social-historical moments are thus overdetermined inasmuch as various heterogeneous and contradictory beliefs, agendas, imperatives and systems or institutions coexist. This state of overdetermined social relations for Althusser (who draws on Lenin as well as Mao) is represented most starkly in the dialectical contradiction between labour and capital and is further articulated in his thinking on **ideology**. Moreover, Althusser's structural-materialist analysis and understanding of overdetermination demonstrates how the concept is specifically historical in that specific forms and circumstances are organised differently from period to period.

P

Palimpsest—Any writing surface on which an earlier writing has been erased or effaced and a later writing inscribed or overlaid on that surface, often with the traces of the former inscription appearing underneath.

Panopticon—Though originally an optical instrument or device, the word has entered critical discourse through Michel Foucault's appropriation of the term from the writings of Jeremy Bentham, who employed it to define circular prison structures, with cells arranged around a central courtyard in which prisoners can be observed at all times. Foucault extends the idea of the panopticon to include a number of social forms of surveillance in hospitals, asylums and so on.

Parapraxis—Freudian term, denoting inadvertent slips of the tongue or pen as revealed symptoms of psychic disturbance; the **subject** or analysand, intending to say or write one thing, says or writes something else which has been repressed.

Paradigm—A pattern, model or exemplary case.

Parody—A written imitation of an author's work, following closely the tone or style of the original, but reworked so as to produce comic or inappropriate effect.

Pathetic fallacy—Term coined by John Ruskin to signify the attribution of nature with human emotions and qualities, or the **displacement** of a psychic condition onto natural phenomena such as atmospherics.

Patriarchy—Literally 'the rule of the father'. Patriarchy is the name given to the whole complex system of male dominance by which most societies are run now and were run in the past. Patriarchy includes the systematic exclusion of women from rights of inheritance, to education, the vote, equal pay, equal rights before the law; it also includes the ways in which even more liberal regimes tend to leave women out of structures of **power** even when they claim to be regimes based on equality.

Performance/performative—The act of public exhibition that results in a transaction between performer and audience; an utterance that, via its public display, causes a linguistic interaction with the exhibition's object. The condition of performative articulation is given particular consideration by Jacques Derrida in the context of the instability of speech acts. Derrida's analysis of the performative in 'Signature Event Context' comes as a response to the work of speech act theorist J. L. Austin, who distinguishes between constative and performative or illocutionary utterances, the former being an 'assertion' or 'description', the latter being an 'utterance which allows us to do something by means of speech itself'. In *Bodies that Matter: On the Discursive Limits of Sex* (1993), Judith Butler identifies performative speech acts as 'forms of authoritative speech: most performatives, for instance, are statements that, in the uttering, also perform a certain action and exercise a binding power'. Derrida's critique, on which Butler draws, is built on his understanding that an utterance is never stable but always available for citation and iterability and, indeed, only aspires to communicability in being transmissible, repeatable, beyond its supposedly 'original' **context** (which itself is never self-sufficient). Thus the idea of a speech act as act is already troubled by the iterable condition of the sign.

Performative speech act—(see **constative speech act**).

Perlocutionary speech act—(see **constative speech act**).

Phallic—Relating to or resembling the phallus, a symbol of generative power; refers to an interest in the phallus or a masculinist point of view; in psychoanalysis, a reference to particular stage in male development when the **subject** is preoccupied with the genitals.

Phallic primacy—Concept often associated with Freud's castration complex, phallic primacy refers to the presence of male genitalia and its impact upon psychosocial relations.

Phallocentrism—Privileging of a masculinist, specifically unitary, singular, point of view in terms of individuals, institutions or cultures. Certain strands of feminist criticism aim to offer critiques exposing the phallocentric assumptions of a text. Such feminist criticism examines the ways in which phallocentrism, most fundamentally organised around the **binary opposition** of man/woman, operates through an economy of sexual **difference** which is hierarchical rather than equivalent in relationship.

Phallocratism—The institutionalisation and **hegemony** of a masculinist perspective; in the parlance of French feminist Luce Irigaray, phallocratism refers to the often masculinised division of labour that exists between the sexes.

Phallogocentrism—Neologism, coined by Jacques Derrida, in order to suggest how logocentric thought or discourse (see **logocentrism**), in being organised around a supposedly central truth or concept, is also phallocentric (see **phallic; phallocentrism**); that is to say, it orientates itself and its subjects to that centre as the sole centre or implied origin, presence or authority from which all other terms, concepts and ideas derive their meaning, whether semantically, epistemologically or theologically.

Phantasm—A mental image, the product of **fantasy**, the imagination or delusion; imaginary projections or visualisations, images arising from the unconscious. Louis Althusser observes in his reading of the Freudian concept of the phantasm that, inasmuch as the phantasm is a figure for **desire**, it thus operates metaphorically.

Phenomenology—Philosophical discourse founded by German philosopher Edmund Husserl that maintains that objects attain meaning through their perception in a given person's **consciousness**.

Philology—Though rarely used in this sense now, philology signifies the love of literature; more broadly, it referred to the study, interpretation and criticism of literature, though this meaning is now also rare.

Phoneme—The basic sound unit of pronunciation in language; English, for example, includes 45 phonemes.

Phonocentrism—Neologism coined by Jacques Derrida in *Of Grammatology*, by which he identifies the tendency in philosophy and linguistics to privilege speech and the voice as guarantors of truth and presence, self-presence and self-consciousness over writing, which signifies absence and may be open to misinterpretation.

Pleasure/pleasure principal—Pleasure refers to a state of gratification, particularly in terms of delight or sensual fulfilment. Freud names the pleasure principle the psychic drive after gratification which has to be repressed in order that humans can function in the social world. Jacques Lacan develops a distinction between pleasure and *jouissance*, with the pleasure principle naming a symbolic law which, in Lacan's words, 'regulates the whole functioning of the psychic apparatus'. *Jouissance*, on the other hand, is disruptive rather than regulatory.

Pluralism—Variety of approach and assumption. A pluralist approach to criticism is one that has many different methods and assumptions at its disposal, rather than an approach that imposes a single model on all texts, no matter what the circumstances. What is significant about critical pluralism is that the various positions which any pluralist discourse brings together are not significantly at odds with one another, and that pluralism often signals an implicit, if not explicit, consensus.

Point de capiton—Phrase employed by Jacques Lacan, usually translated as 'quilting', 'anchoring' or 'suturing' point. Taken from embroidery, the phrase indicates for Lacan moments in the psyche where signifier and signified are gathered, or stitched together, thereby momentarily bringing to a halt the slippage of signification by which **subjectivity** is constituted.

Polysemy—Relating to the possibility of a simultaneous multiplicity of meaning encoded within a single phrase or text.

Positivism—Philosophical theory, formulated by Auguste Comte, which privileges observable facts and phenomena over modes of knowledge such as theology and metaphysics.

'Post'—The notion – as signalled in terms such as post-modernism, postmarxism, poststructuralism or post-theory – of an intellectual moment that ensues after the occurrence of a paradigm shift or **epistemological** transition of sorts. In addition to denoting the pastness of a given intellectual or cultural epoch, 'post' suggests the persistence of enduring philosophical quandaries and discoveries associated with such historical or theoretical moments, which the notion of 'postism' hints are not, in fact, over but which haunt or disturb the progressivist sense of having apparently moved beyond particular modes of enquiry.

Postmodernism—There is little general consensus concerning the meaning of the term, and its use and history is chequered. Its earliest appearances date back to the first decades of the twentieth century, as critics such as Perry Anderson and Fredric Jameson discuss in their work on postmodernism. It has also been used extensively in the field of architecture as the name for a school or movement. With reference to literature and culture, 'postmodernism' is often taken to refer to any work of art which knowingly refers to its own status as a work of art, or which otherwise, from the position as elite art form, jokingly addresses the status of the art object through construction from or reference to popular culture, thereby collapsing distinctions between high and low.

However, certain theorists of the postmodern, such as Fredric Jameson, Jean-François Lyotard and Teresa Ebert find the problematic of defining postmodernism a question of its being a product of particular political **overdeterminations**, which serve to produce postmodernism's often apparently contradictory meanings, and whereby the postmodern condition is fundamentally misrecognised in **aesthetic** terms. The meaning or identity of the postmodern is understood, then, as a self-conscious aesthetic component of its constitution, rather than as a political effect of late-twentieth-century global capitalism. There is therefore a shift in definition from the formalist aesthetic radicalism perceived by William Spanos, for example, to a more politically or **ideologically** comprehended aspect to what we call postmodernism.

Postmodernity—Term referring to the era, state of being or literary arts associated with **postmodernism**. Jean-François Lyotard defines postmodernity as being marked by a suspicion of **grand narratives**. The idea of a postmodern era is also one provisionally defined by the advent of **tele-technologies**, the emergence of globalisation and post-industrial society, and the power of the image and **simulacrum** within consumer culture, where images such as the Coke or Nike logos assume greater significance in themselves than any real product or reality to which they might refer.

Power—In the work of Michel Foucault, power constitutes one of the three axes constitutive of **subjectification**, the other two being **ethics** and truth. For Foucault, power implies knowledge, and vice versa. However, power is causal, it is constitutive of knowledge, even while knowledge is, concomitantly, constitutive of power: knowledge gives one power, but one has the power in given circumstances to constitute bodies of knowledge, discourses and so on as valid or invalid, truthful or untruthful. Power serves in making the world both knowable and controllable. Yet, the nature of power, as Foucault suggests, is essentially proscriptive, concerned more with imposing limits on its subjects.

Praxis—Term adopted by Karl Marx in 1844 to denote social activity by which political theory or philosophy becomes social and historical actuality.

Presentism—Refers to a radical over-emphasis or privileging of the present over what is perceived to be a less culturally and technologically effectual past.

Primal horde/scene—That which is primal refers in Freudian psychoanalysis to the **desires**, fears, needs and anxieties, constitutive of the origins of the **subject's** psyche. The idea of the primal horde signifies an originary human social collective. The primal scene is that moment in Freudianism when the infant subject becomes aware of sexual relations between its parents.

Projection—In psychoanalytic discourse, the transference of **desire** or **fantasy** onto another person, object or situation, in order to avoid the recognition of the **subject's** responsibility for his or her behaviour or actions.

Prosopopoeia—Literally meaning 'to make or give face', a rhetorical figure by which an abstract idea or concept is given human form, or otherwise the representation of an imaginary or absent person as if he or she were speaking.

Pseudo-statement—Concept often associated with British formalist I. A. Richards which refers to a spurious utterance dominated by emotion and lacking in referential truth; according to Richards, such a statement finds its origins in human impulses and attitudes, rather than in generally accepted notions of truth.

Q

Queer—Term often associated with the contemporary gay and lesbian studies movement, i.e. queer theory (this identification, it should be noted, registering a significant development from, or even, in some cases, break with, the idea of gay and lesbian studies). Queer denotes a sense of **otherness**, as well as a means for breaking with convention and theorising about sexuality and its significant place in the construction of transcultural models of homosexuality. 'Queer' has been deployed as an affirmative and performative term which resists becoming a fixed category and thus gives voice to those elided or marginalised by 'gay' and 'lesbian' studies: bisexuals, transexuals, sado-masochists, for example. It is thus the very identificatory slipperiness in the term which maintains its political potential. Judith Butler argues that it is in the **iterable** mutability of *queer*'s semantic operation that it can operate most effectively. Only while the term resists being domesticated, Butler argues, will it remain strategically, critically and, most importantly, politically efficacious.

R

Race—At its broadest, race refers to a family, tribe, people or nation sharing a set of common interests, beliefs, habits or characteristics. However, pre-eminent African American literary and cultural critic Henry Louis Gates alerts the reader to a number of important details concerning the thinking and reading of race. To begin with, to speak of different 'races', such as 'black' or 'Jewish' is, says Gates, to 'speak in biological misnomers and, more generally, metaphors.' Despite this error, such usage persists in both everyday language and in literary texts. What the idea of race and its mobilisation point to for Gates is the articulation of a sense of **difference** which is dynamic inasmuch as '"race" has both described and *inscribed* differences of language, belief system, artistic tradition, and gene pool, as well as all sorts of supposedly natural attributes such as rhythm, athletic ability, cerebration, usury, fidelity, and so forth . . . Race has become a trope of ultimate, irreducible difference between cultures, linguistic groups, or adherents of specific belief systems'. Thus, as a discursive, political and ideological term, race functions frequently as a means of definition based on **binary oppositions** between self and other, civilised and savage, and so on.

Richard Dyer has argued that in many cultural and historical instances, racial imagery has relied on the assumption that non-white people are 'raced', as he puts it, while white people supposedly are not, or do not see themselves in racial terms, unless believing themselves to be threatened by racial difference. As Dyer puts it, '[t]he sense of whites as non-racial is most evident in the absence of reference to whiteness in the habitual speech and writing of white people in the West.' From this, it is not too great a leap, Dyer contends, to say 'that white people are just people, which is not far off from saying that whites are people whereas other colours are something else'. Colour thus becomes a visible sign of apparent racial identity. Racial attitudes of this kind are, therefore, one particularly crude articulation of **ethnocentrism**. Questions of race involve matters of identity and difference, the determination of humanity and (implicitly if not explicitly) what constitutes civilisation and matters of representation, specifically corporeal representation allied to discourses on race. Non-white peoples are all too frequently reduced in cultural representations, in texts and films, to stereotypes where race signifies an **overdetermined** generation of meaning bringing together corporeality and behaviour or custom, as though there were some logical connection between these.

At its broadest and most neutral, according to Dyer, race 'is a means of categorising different types of human body which reproduce themselves. It seeks to systematise differences and to relate them to differences of character and worth'. There are two principal approaches to racial categorisation: genealogical and biological. The former concerns itself with notions of origin and heritage, while the latter interests itself in anatomical and corporeal differences. In genealogical narrations, Caucasian and Aryan groups are privileged as the apex of racial development, intrinsic to which narratives is the search for founding moments and the desire for racial purity.

Modern definitions of race frequently emerge coterminously with national, **colonial** and ethnocentric **discourses** and practices. From the early modern period onwards most notably, racial difference is determined in the assumption of physical similarities and allegedly shared characteristics of temperament, supposedly discernible as common to groups of people living in a particular geographical domain.

Rationalism—Refers to the reliance upon reason as the basis for establishing religious or philosophical truth. In addition, philosophical notion, deriving from the work of Descartes, which emphasises the constitution of knowledge, based on reason rather than observation or sense perception.

Reader/reading—A reader can be provisionally defined as a person who evaluates intellectually a given manuscript or image in an effort to comprehend or interpret its contents or form for a range of reasons, whether these reasons are defined as 'entertainment', 'education', 'enlightenment', 'pleasure' or a combination of these and other purposes. What we call reading is an active participation with a piece of writing or an image for the purpose of producing meaning, or, more generally, to 'translate' the book or image (or, indeed, the world) from its condition as a perceived ensemble of potential signs to a **text** on which the process of interpretation is brought to bear. It is important, if seemingly obvious, to note that reading takes time; the analysis of signs does not occur immediately, even if the object of reading is a poster or advertisement in a magazine. Reading is thus engaged in as a temporal experience, an experience which is not limited to the time of holding the book open, standing in front of an image or watching a film (whether in the cinema or on a video). Moreover, reading is never simple or innocent, even when one reads 'for pleasure', as the phrase has it, because the reader, any reader, is always positioned through culture, history, education, **ideology** and so on. Thus the possibility of reading is constituted in various ways prior to any individual act of reading. At the same time, every text has a **singularity** for which the act of reading should be responsible and to which the act of reading should respond. One should therefore avoid producing a reading which is either, on the one hand, simply a passive consumption or, on the other, the active imposition of a particular meaning which suppresses or excludes other elements. Such a reading might be a 'politicised' reading which, in its address of matters of class representation ignores issues of gender or race. Or, there is the formal reading which, in discussing the **aesthetic** aspects of the writing ignores or downplays the roles of history or ideology, of the function of **epistemological** assumptions behind the value judgements which the text appears to advance or which we, as readers, bring to the text. How one reads is therefore irreducible to a prescription or formula because of singularity and the responsibility to that singularity which reading entails. In the light of the question of singularity, some critics have suggested that to impose a 'reading' along certain lines (the political, the purely formal) is to avoid the complex negotiation that reading involves; it is the imposition of a reading within limits and towards a limit or horizon (this being the 'political', 'philosophical' or 'historical' meaning which is sought), and is, therefore, not a reading at all, but the avoidance of reading. At the same time, however, the responsibility of reading is such that one cannot simply read as one likes; one has to be attentive to the ways in which the text is articulated, the ways in which it appears to articulate itself and the ways in which it appears to be silent on matters. There is, furthermore, in the act of reading the experience of the **undecidable**. For these reasons, properly speaking the act of reading cannot come to an end. Reading always remains to come, not as a future moment or horizon in itself at which textual explication will arrive eventually, and therefore have done with reading, but as the responsibility of the encounter with **singularity, undecidability** and **otherness**.

Realism/realist—Realism has many meanings and is potentially an unusable word since people differ over what they mean by reality. In literature and the arts, however, it describes a common tendency from the early nineteenth century onwards to represent real life in fiction and painting, and to do so using common conventions of representation. One of the key problems with the term, though, is that nineteenth-century realist writers were generally ruthlessly selective in their materials, presenting not so much real life in the raw, but reality filtered and purged. Realism is often associated with representing average experience – the lives of middle-class characters who do little that is unusual or exciting; it prefers an objective standpoint, and is illusionist in that it asks its readers to forget that they are reading fiction. Readers are meant to 'identify' with characters as if they were real people. Events should be probable (or at the very least, possible); narrators should on the whole maintain a third-person distance and perspective; judgement should be easy for the reader. These conventions have become natur-alised in many people's reading habits so that it is often difficult to disentangle reality from its representation. None-theless, many critics have attacked **bourgeois** realism for its narrow focus, moral certainties and social exclusivity.

Reality principle/effect—Term often associated with Jean Bau-drillard that relates to the ways in which reality is often established and becomes represented for some individuals and cultures through **hyperreal** media such as photography, film and other media.

Referent—In **Saussurean linguistics**, the referent is that to which the word or sign refers: the real object in the real world for which the word or sign is an arbitrary and conventional signal.

Referential—A text that is referential is one that disguises its status as a work or text by making extended reference to the conditions of real life. The reader, that is, is encouraged to forget that what he or she is reading is *merely* a text.

Reflection—Term employed in certain early strands of marxist analysis which sees a simple one-to-one relationship between **base** and **superstructure** or, in literary terms, **text** and world.

Reification—The process or result of rendering some idea or philosophy into a material or concrete entity. The process by which philosophical or **ideological** concepts disappear to the extent that they become incorporated into the everyday. Concept employed in marxist discourse which emphasises the depersonalisation of the **subject** as a result of **capitalist** modes of production and the **alienation** of labour.

Repetition compulsion—The neurotic and often harmful psychological condition in which the afflicted continue to engage in patterns of self-destructive and dangerous behaviour.

Repression—In psychoanalytic thought, repression is the process by which **subjects** try to get rid of **desires**, linked to instincts and imaged in thoughts and memory, that are somehow known to be forbidden by the wider culture. The forbidden thoughts are consigned to the **Unconscious**; but they do not disappear, and may manifest themselves in symptomatic behaviours, in dreams, slips of the tongue and physical tics. Such symptoms are examples of what Freud called 'the return of the repressed'.

Rhetoric—The study of the art of speaking or writing effectively, as well as a skill involving the correct usage of speech. Rhetoric similarly refers to a given mode of language or aspect of verbal communication.

Rhizome—The figure of the rhizome, which is taken from a form of continuous, underground plant stem growth consisting of lateral shoots, is adapted strategically by Gilles Deleuze and Félix Guattari. It suggests for Deleuze and Guattari a non-formalisable figure for thinking differently so as to affirm and potentialise the constant **becoming** of a thinking which **deterritorialises** the boundaries of conventional thinking within disciplines.

Romanticism—The literary term that refers to the literary, artistic and general culture of the first half of the nineteenth century. Romanticism is distinguished by its general embrace of the emotions and nature, particularly in response to a growing sense of materialism and to such moments of violence and upheaval as the French Revolution of 1789. In addition to rejecting the forms and conventions often associated with classicism and neoclassicism, romanticists sought value in spontaneity, subjective experience and original expression.

S

Saussurean linguistics—A linguistic model deriving from the lectures of Ferdinand de Saussure. Saussure argued that the meanings that we give to words are not intrinsic but arbitrary; there is no connection between a word and its meaning except the one that we choose to give it. He further suggested that meanings are also relational. If a word has no inherent connection with its meaning, then its meaning derives from relations to do with **context** and syntax. Thirdly, Saussure also argued that language constitutes our reality: since our only access to meaning is through language, language itself must form us and our thoughts, not the other way around. His interest in language was to study the linguistic system (or **Langue**) rather than the individual utterance (or Parole) in order to understand the complete picture of human language, an approach taken up by structuralist theory which concentrates on larger structures.

Schizoanalysis—Term associated with the work of Gilles Deleuze and Félix Guattari. Schizoanalysis is opposed to the normative imperative in psychoanalysis embodied in the idea of the cure. As an analytical discourse, it aims to **deterritorialise** the discourses of the individual within an Oedipal schema, and to read various flows of **desire** irreducible to the imposition of limiting structures on the **self**. Schizoanalysis announces such flows as lines of escape, Deleuze and Guattari seeking to construct a critical discourse which itself escapes such limiting notions as the 'human', and the situation of the 'proper' human **subject** within economic frameworks such as the Oedipal. Schizoanalysis is described as a radical political and social form of psychoanalysis which extends beyond the traditional territory of psychoanalysis, the family. Through this Deleuze and Guattari propose to connect desire to **capitalism**'s effects in particular ways, defining so-called human drives as the work of **desiring machines** while also proposing, in their words, 'to demonstrate the existence of an unconscious libidinal investment of sociohistorical production, distinct from the conscious investments coexisting with it'.

Scopophilia—The (often sexualised) pleasure in looking. Feminist critics in particular have criticised Freud's theories of infantile sexuality for their scopophilic emphasis on 'looking' and seeing the (**absence or presence** of the) sexual organs of the other sex. Feminist film theory, following the work of

Laura Mulvey and influenced by Lacanian psychoanalysis, has theorised the **gaze** – that of both the camera and the audience – in terms of a scopophilic drive.

Screen memories—In Freudian theory, fragments of memories that substitute for forgotten or repressed childhood sexual memories.

Selective tradition—Term coined by Raymond Williams to denote how a cultural heritage, apparently bequeathed to the present by the past, is in fact constructed in the present through processes of active selection.

Self—The psychological or cultural conception of a given individual's identity or sense of human particularity.

Self-referentiality—A self-referential text is one that refers to its own processes of production – a text that talks about its textuality. Unlike the referential text, it encourages its readers continually to recall that what is being read is fictive or illusory, not real at all.

Semantic field—A linguistic term for defining an area of perception or experience as this is structured or overdetermined by interrelated terms, phrases and words.

Semiology—Analysis of linguistic signs; coined by Swiss linguist Ferdinand de Saussure in the early twentieth century as the linguistic study of socially and culturally inscribed codes of human interaction.

Semiotic/s—In the plural, semiotics refers to the 'science of signs' – systematic codes of representation. Julia Kristeva, however, has coined the term 'the Semiotic' to refer to a mode in language. Language, she says, consists of the Symbolic (derived from Lacan), the linguistic realm of transparency, paraphrasability, conformity and power. The Semiotic is the pre-linguistic residue of language, made up of sounds, rhythms, the babbling incoherence of the child, the language of poetry and the language of psychosis. It is not precisely meaningless, but it cannot be subsumed in the Symbolic. The Semiotic pulses against Symbolic language, making it mean both more and less than it intends.

Sexual difference—The differences between the sexes that derive from their different biological sex organs; by extension, sexual difference in psychoanalysis and other theories is also shown to have cultural and psychic effects beyond the merely bodily.

Sexuality—A mobile concept, not easily contained through definition. If we follow the work of Elizabeth Grosz, it is possible to define sexuality in four different ways: (a) as a psychoanalytic drive; (b) as a constellation of practices 'involving bodies, organs and pleasures'; (c) as an identity which is culturally and psychically assumed and projected, and closely related to concepts and constructions of **gender**; (d) as a 'set of orientations, positions, and **desires**'. To this schema we can add that, in ordinary language, sexuality simply refers to sexual practice, to the performance in various ways of desire. In literary and cultural theory, however, the word is much more complex and contested. For Freud, sexuality refers to the attempts to achieve desired objects, whether or not these desires are self-evidently sexual or not. In Freudian terms, **masculine** sexuality is defined by competitiveness and aggression; **feminine** sexuality by lack (of the phallus) and passivity. The achievement of gendered sexuality is the prerequisite for the achievement of maturity. For other writers, most notably Michel Foucault, sexuality is the placing of sexual practice into the realm of discourse; sexuality is not so much 'what we do' as 'how we describe what we do', and the conditions culturally and socially by which the ways in which we describe become shaped and so determine our articulations (the types of words we use, in what **contexts**, how the terms change according to context, the associations of pleasure or guilt with the discourse). Furthermore, Foucault argues that such descriptions are always necessarily implicated in the formation and use of **power**. In much feminist writing, there has been a re-vision of Freudian analysis, especially in relation to feminine sexuality. Writers such as Luce Irigaray and Hélène Cixous have argued that feminine sexuality is not reducible to a series of simple formulae (lack and passivity); instead feminine sexuality is to be understood as multiple, flowing and unlimitable. This model is proposed partly in order to re-evaluate the question of female creativity against male-ordained versions of a femininity that cannot be active in its own behalf, and which is not defined by pleasure (or **jouissance**).

Sexuate—Term associated with French feminist Luce Irigaray's notion of suppressed maternal womanhood.

Sign—According to C. S. Peirce, a sign, or *representamen*, is 'something that stands to somebody for something in some respect or capacity'. Peirce demonstrated the nature of a given sign's attributes via such concepts as **mediation** and triadicity. Peirce argues that signs are invariably mediated by the external forces of history, culture and time, and these mediating entities characterise the ways in which we interpret signs and symbols. The process of triadicity finds its origins in the dyadic relationship between the sign itself and the signified, which refers to the idea that constitutes the sign's meaning. Peirce furthered this notion in terms of a more complex, triadic relationship between the sign and the signified, as well as between the sign and the interpretant, which Peirce described as 'all that is explicit in the sign itself apart from its context and circumstances of utterance'. For Peirce, signs become actualised when they represent something other than themselves. Signs exist as mere objects when standing on their own. In other words, signs always depend upon something other than themselves to establish their uniqueness. In Peirce's philosophy, then, signs are inevitably subordinate to their qualities of representation. Essentially, signs can only be recognised in a relational **context** with something other than themselves; hence, signs take on their unique characteristics of being when interpreted in terms of their historical or cultural antecedents. According to Saussure, a sign comprises a sound image, or signifier, and a concept, or signified. The signifier refers to a set of speech sounds in language, while the signified functions as the meaning that undergirds the sign itself. Eschewing Peirce's theories regarding the objectivity and subjectivity of language, Saussure's semiology contends that the senses of identity or uniqueness of all aspects of language emerge via the **differences** inherent in that language's network of linguistic relationships rather than through a given langua-ge's objective features. This concept demonstrates Saussure's paradoxical argument that in a given language system mean-ing is generated only through difference between signifiers. There are no positive terms or signs the meaning of which is self-sufficient.

Signification—Relates generally to Ferdinand de Saussure's con-ception of the sign, which consists of two inseparable as-pects, the signifier and the signified.

Signifier/signified—Saussure argues that a word or image (the sign) comes in two parts. There is the sound it makes (or its graphic equivalent) which he terms the 'signifier'; and there is the mental image that the sound or graphic equivalent produces in the reader/viewer – the signified. The relation-ship between signifier and signified is entirely arbitrary and conventional; it is 'however' also impossible to separate the two. Furthermore, the relationship between the sign in its constituent parts of signifier/signified and its referent (the real object to which it refers) is also arbitrary. In other words, signified and referent are not interchangeable terms for Saussure.

Simulacra/simulacrum/simulation—Term often associated with Jean Baudrillard's notion of the **reality effect,** which relates to the ways in which reality is often established and becomes replaced for some individuals and cultures through hyperreal media such as photography, film and other media; hence, simulacrum refers to the image, representation or reproduc-tion of a concrete other in which the very idea of the real is no longer the signified of which the simulacrum is the signified. Simulation, the process whereby simulacra assume their function, belongs to what Baudrillard terms the 'second order': there is no anterior 'real', the idea of the 'real' only coming into being through the cultural dissemination of images (such as those of advertising) or simulacra.

Singularity—Jacques Derrida postulates that our understanding of every sign involves an assumption of the absolute singularity, the uniqueness of that sign or mark, that is to say, its singularity. However, for it to be possible for the sign to communicate or have meaning, it has to be transmissible, reiterable. It therefore cannot be absolutely singular. Yet, paradoxically, the possibility of inscription outside of any finite or determinable **context** – in order to function properly as my name, my proper name must be able to be transmissible outside my presence – while denying absolute singularity, also suggests the singularity which apparently gives the sign its **authority**. The term is employed by Jean-Luc Nancy to describe a given individual's particularity, or the essence that establishes and maintains their irreducible sense of **self**, with the proviso that any sense of self, subjectivity or **being** is also, always, a being-with, or being-in-common.

Sinthome—Lacanian term meaning symptom; the spelling of the word is archaic. For Lacan, the symptom is a radical signifier of the unconscious irreducible to any interpretation or meaning.

Social construction—Concept that explains the ways in which ideas, identities and texts result from the interaction among socialised norms of existence, cultural politics and individualised senses of identity.

Solipsism—The belief that one can only ever have proper evidence of one's own existence; an absolute egotism which depends on refusing to admit the existence, demands and needs of others.

Speaking (as) woman (parler-femme)—Term employed by Luce Irigaray indicative of experimental modalities of writing, implicitly stressing Irigaray's understanding of the relation between writing and female sexuality and disruptive of univocal syntaxes and logic.

Speech-act theory—A theory of language established by British philosopher John L. Austin, who believed in contextualising language study. Austin's theories rejected the prevailing notions that all possible sentences are basic or *kernel* sentences and that such sentences declare something that can be determined to be either true or false. Austin defined verbal utterances as either constatives or performatives. According to Austin, constatives refer to something that can be determined to be either true or false, while performatives denote sentences that engage in such activities as questioning, admonishing or pleading.

Story/plot—In broad terms, the story is the combined details or facts of a narrative; the plot is the organisation and emphasis that shapes the story and its reception, and the order or sequence in which the details or facts are given.

Stream of consciousness—Literary technique, in which the consciousness of the narrator or narrated subject's consciousness is represented freed from logical order or the demands of external narrative events. The language of the subject's conscious is articulated as a flow of inner experience and mediation.

Structure of feeling—Term coined by Raymond Williams as a mediating concept between 'art' and 'culture' to denote the 'deep community' that makes communication possible. A structure of feeling is neither universal nor class specific, but 'a very deep and wide possession'. The term was meant to embrace both the immediately experiential and the generationally-specific aspects of artistic process.

Subaltern—Term, taken from the work of Antonio Gramsci and used initially to define proletarian and other working-class groups, *subaltern* is employed in postcolonial studies after Gayatri Spivak to address dominated and marginalised groups.

Subject position—The location in a text identified as that belonging to the human **subject,** or the assumed position within a text that is identified as its 'voice'.

Subculture—Specific cultural group within larger cultures sharing specific interests or values. Cultural critic Dick Hebdige defines subcultures according to shared symbolic use of styles in clothing, music, speech and so on, often in deliberate opposition to dominant or mainstream cultural ideologies.

Subject/subjectivity—The concept of selfhood that is developed in and articulated through the acquisition of language. A subject is a **self** in language; subjectivity is the process of attaining and expressing selfhood in and through language or the location of the self situated and subjectified by cultural, **epistemological, ideological** and other social discourses and institutions.

Sublimation—A Freudian term, sublimation signifies the ways in which sexual drives are rerouted into other creative and intellectual areas of activity which are socially acceptable.

Sublime—An **aesthetic** category, that which in a work of art which produces responses of awe and strong emotion. Most if not all of the current discourses of the sublime in critical thinking are inherited or developed, directly or otherwise, from commentaries of the concept of the sublime in the eighteenth century, as that concept came to be elaborated in relation to matters of taste, **empirical** psychology, the discourse of the landscape and related philosophical considerations. While it is the work of Edmund Burke which has traditionally been considered as constituting the principal consideration of the sublime, this is by no means the only discussion to be taken into account. Much recent theoretical work which addresses the question of the sublime, and the ways in which analysis of aesthetic effect is tied to human perception and the constitution of the **subject**, has returned to Immanuel Kant's profound analysis of the sublime.

Superego—According to Freud, the moral or judicial aspect of the psyche; the superego is transferred from parents to children and acts as a moral censor through the re-enforcement of social standards and norms of 'acceptable' or so called 'normal' behaviour.

Supplement/supplementarity—Quasi-concept which, as Jacques Derrida points out, means both an addition and a replacement, developed in response to Rousseau's understanding of writing as a supplement to speech. The idea of supplementarity puts into play the disruption of a full presence of a sign in making possible signification, indicating the work of **difference** within the self-same. The supplement is supposed to act as an addition or complement which completes. In so doing, the supplement is meant to cover up a lack, but, in being a supplement, in producing the meaning of the 'original', it disrupts the very idea of the original as self-sufficient.

Suture—Term in Lacanian psychoanalysis describing the moment that a given **subject** enters into language; hence, the suture denotes the linguistic gap that the subject subsumes within a given language.

Symbolic institution—Term often associated with Slavoj Žižek that refers to the ways in which individuals or cultures attempt to manipulate their conventional, more socially or politically relevant others by enacting artificial systems of thought or organisation in their places.

Symbolism—The usage of symbols in order to represent other things, ideas or concepts. In literary works, symbolism refers to an author's attempt to create a series of associations and incremental or applied meanings. Symbolism also refers to the late nineteenth-century French literary movement that rejected literary realism in favour of subjective symbols that evoke emotional reactions among readers.

Symptomatic reading—Refers to a kind of reading practice that accounts for the **power**/knowledge relations that exist when the notion of meaning is in intellectual or ideological conflict; symptomatic readers reconstruct a given text's discursive conditions in order to treat the text as a symptom, understand its internal relations and comprehend – by challenging the text's intellectual properties – the ways in which it ultimately produces (or fails to produce) meaning.

Synecdoche—A figure of speech in which the part is substituted for the whole, or the whole for the part; thus 'four sails', meaning 'four ships'.

Syntagm—Term often associated with Roman Jakobson that refers to an orderly combination of interacting signifiers that establish a meaningful whole; in language, for example, a sentence functions as a syntagm of words.

$\boxed{\text{T}}$

Technoscience—Term often associated with Paul Virilio that refers to the ubiquitous ways in which technological culture and the information world dominate social, political, and economic spheres of influence.

Tekhne—From the Greek for 'making', but also defined by Heidegger as a 'bringing forth'; Heidegger argues that *tekhne* is most appropriately understood not as or in the act of manual production so much as what is revealed by the act of making. A general term pertaining to any technical rather than essential determination in the broadest sense of technique, relating to technology, **writing** (in Derrida's sense), artistic technique and so forth, in opposition to essence or substance, to which technique is traditionally or metaphysically subordinated as at best an auxiliary means. The term is usually used, primarily following Heidegger and Derrida, to indicate, by contrast, the equally constitutive rather than subordinate role of *tekhne* and, by so doing, to enable a more general deconstruction of the metaphysics of presence.

Tele-technology—Refers to all electronic media such as the Internet, video, e-mail, television, telephony and the general thought of the system to which these belong, by which images, messages, signals and signs, discourses, etc. are transmitted and circulated.

Telos/teleology—Telos refers to any form of ultimate end or conclusion; teleology denotes the study of the role of design in nature and an attempt to explain the existence of natural phenomena.

Text/textuality—Since the work of Roland Barthes and other critics who are associated with the terms structuralism and poststructuralism, the term *text* has taken on the sense of a process rather than a finished product, of which books and other literary forms are examples. A novel may be a text, but textuality is not confined by the idea of the book. Textuality thus names the interwoven discourses, phenomena or other grouping of signs, images and so forth by which we perceive the world and by which we, as **subjects**, are situated.

Theatre of cruelty—Phrase coined by playwright Antonin Artaud, intended to define plays that communicate human suffering and evil via the staged presentation of extremities of violence.

Theory—A very loosely wielded term which has become somewhat vacuous, at least potentially so, 'theory' refers, in the field of literary studies, to the critical movement which has emerged in the Anglo-American university since the 1960s as a response in large part to interest within the English-speaking academic world in particular strands of continental linguistics, **narratology**, psychoanalysis, **semiotics** and philosophy. What is termed theory is often associated with equally diffuse terms such as poststructuralism in which literary theorists have attempted to establish new spheres of learning and new approaches to canonical and noncanonical texts alike. Such approaches might best be defined, albeit warily, as certain momentary hybrid coalitions or assemblages of **epistemological** and **ontological** interests, a rethinking of the historical, the constitution of **subjectivity** and sexuality, and the political and philosophical grounds of **narrative** and representation.

Thick description—Term coined by anthropologist Clifford Geertz, describing the complex layering and overdetermination of any cultural or social event.

Topos—Theme, motif, convention or recurring rhetorical device.

Trace—Jacques Derrida formulates the idea of the trace as what remains when an instance of **singularity**, such as a signature, has erased the possibility of its absolute singularity in having been inscribed. The trace is the mark of that which has never been present or presentable as such. The trace makes meaning possible by being, for Derrida, the *différance* which disrupts any notion of absolute origin. Jean Baudrillard's use of the term refers to the trace of meaning that the reality effect fosters; arguing that postmodernity has resulted in an artificial era of hyperreality, Baudrillard explains the notion of trace as a kind of nostalgia via which we establish meaning in our lives.

Tradition—A socially or culturally established, inherited or customary pattern of thought, action or behaviour. Tradition also refers to a characteristic manner, method or style of organisation or conduct.

Transference—Psychoanalytic term indicating the process by which the analysand transfers and thereby repeats the psychic dynamic developed in early childhood pertaining to **desire** of the other onto the analyst.

Transgression—Generally, the act of breaking a law, or of overstepping, crossing, a boundary or limit, one which is usually socially, institutionally or conventionally defined and applied. Michel Foucault develops the concept and thinking of transgression as practical critique of the limits of forms of knowledge in specific ways relating to the **subject's** freedom. Foucault points out the interdependency of the concepts of the limit and transgression. There could be no idea of the limit unless it were crossable, at least in principle. However, the duration of transgression in relation to the limit is very brief: for, as Foucault argues, once the act of transgression crosses the limit, the transgression is no longer a transgression, strictly speaking. The importance of the idea of transgression for Foucault is in the fact that, as he puts it, 'transgression forces the limit to face the fact of its imminent disappearance'. The relationship of transgression to the limit thus comprehended is not one of simple **binary opposition** but is, instead, a radically destabilising relationship. For Foucault transgression does not simply oppose; nor is it a negative. Rather, it affirms in a neutral fashion an instance of freedom and limitlessness.

Transparency—The idea that the **narrative** voice in realist fiction does not **mediate** or interpret the world it presents but that it allows direct access to that world in neutral terms.

Trope—Rhetorical **figure** of speech consisting of use of word, term or phrase in a sense other than that which is conventionally proper to it; figurative language.

Typology—A system or scheme of classification based upon a set of principles, concepts or types.

$\boxed{\text{U}}$

Uncanny—Most often associated with the work of Freud but also found in Heidegger's discussion of **Being**, as a fundamental experience of one's being in the world and one's relationship to existence, *uncanny* is the somewhat inaccurate translation from the text of Freud for the German *unheimlich* (lit. unhomely). Freud employs the term in the essay of the same name to signify the feeling of discomfort and strangeness which arises in the **self** without warning. As Freud suggests, the feeling of the uncanny *is* uncanny precisely to the extent that the sensation comes about in places where one should feel most secure, or with which one is most familiar. Freud's use of the German demonstrates how the experience of the uncanny is structural, that is to say how the sense of being 'not-at-home' or 'unhomely' occurs within the idea of the home.

Unconscious—In psychoanalysis, the unconscious is the mental realm into which those aspects of mental life that are related to forbidden **desires** and instincts are consigned through the process of repression. The unconscious is absolutely unknown to the **subject** except where it exerts pressures on conscious life, as when repressed objects refuse to remain repressed. The instincts and desires it contains are usually disguised through a repressive censorship that turns forbidden ideas into different images by the processes of **condensation** and **displacement** (Freud's terms), where they become metonymies and metaphors (Lacan's terms). These censored images seek to re-enter **consciousness** through dreams, symptoms and verbal and physical tics. The subject is unable to interpret the new images him or herself and must submit to analysis to 'read' the pulsions of his or her own unconscious realm.

Undecidability—A term associated with the work of Jacques Derrida, often confused with the idea of indeterminacy. Undecidability persists within structures of meaning, even within particular words, such as the Greek *pharmakon*, which signifies both cure *and* poison, and thereby resists translation into either cure *or* poison. However, undecidability is not simply a matter of equivocation in the etymology of words, even though the doubling and division which inhabits, which spaces, and which makes possible **writing** is seen to belong to the structure of a supposedly originary word. As Derrida shows, the undecidable haunts, and thereby makes impossible, any possible distinction between performative and constative speech acts. For, as Derrida puts it, undecidability 'is not caused by some enigmatic equivocality'. If the undecidable *is* anything, that is to say if we can risk an **ontic** proposition, it is that which marks the movement between ontic or **ontological** definitions and which, in so marking (as the effect of **difference** or writing, or through the strategic use of terms such as *hymen*) any attempted articulation of meaning grounded on the structural separation – and thus, stabilisation – of terms, undermines the very process by which the stable identity or meaning is read. Thus, because of this movement within language and as what remains in language, one cannot complete a 'reading' or make the break with a text that the idea of a reading implies.

Universalism—Refers to the practice of perceiving generalisation in all aspects of human life or intellectual discourse; the **ideology** of making universal assumptions (e.g. concerning 'humanity') which ignores culturally or historically specific or determined aspects of societies, cultures and individuals.

Unreliable narrator—In a novel or short story, a narrator whose perspective is biased, or who is either limited in terms of knowledge or else is psychologically unstable.

Use value/exchange value—The distinction between use and exchange value originated in Aristotle, but was developed and given its modern sense by Marx. Social Theorist Andrew Sayer summarises the difference succinctly: 'Marx insisted on distinguishing capital from mere machines, materials or buildings. The latter have use-value, but only become capital when they are acquired in order to command the labour . . . of others and to earn exchange value'. Thus use-value in marxian terms is restricted to a certain utilitarian instrumentality. Exchange value, on the other hand, implies an aspect of desirability or otherwise a quality where the basic function is subsumed or assumes a secondary position within forms of interchange, interrelation and structural independence. Under capitalism, workers by and large neither work to grow the food they need for sustenance nor do they produce their own clothing and shelter. Instead, they labour for capitalists who own the means of production in order to produce commodities for others to purchase, even as those workers earn money by their labour in turn, in order to buy goods which either they or others have produced. The creation of a commodity, the **commodification** of raw materials into saleable items, for third parties thus typifies the principal of exchange value.

V

Value—The estimation, appraisal or interpretation of a given commodity's worth, significance or utility. Value also refers to a moral principle established by a given individual or community.

W

Writerly and readerly texts—Translations of the French neologisms *scriptible* and *lisible* first employed by Roland Barthes. For Barthes, the readerly or *lisible* text is the most conventional literary work, realist in nature and one which hides the signs of its being a work of fiction or literary production. It is a fixed product, conforming to the dominant cultural modes of literature during the time of its production. Barthes sees such a text as making the reader passive in his or her reception of it, leaving the reader only the choice of either accepting or rejecting it and its ideologically mystified perspective on the world. The writerly or *scriptible* text, on the other hand, draws attention to its own artifice, to the ways in which it is structured, to its intertextuality and its self-reflexivity or self-consciousness, for example, and so challenges the reader to engage actively in the interpretation of such a text.

Writing—Though a familiar enough term indicative of the inscribed marks representing speech, Jacques Derrida explores and expands the term in ways which destabilise the conventional notion of writing as a more or less unproblematic mode of communication, or otherwise as the idea of the graphic approximation of speech. In the essay 'Signature Event Context', Derrida schematises how what he calls the classical concept of writing is usually understood: (a) as a mark which can be reiterated, the function of which is not 'exhausted' in any single inscription. Such a mark, whether in the form of a statement, a signature or proper name, or, indeed, a literary text such as a novel, is, in principal, communicable *as* a writing in that it can communicate beyond and, indeed, before, without, the presence of any living **subject**, such as the author; (b) at the same time, what we call writing may be cited outside its immediate **context** and its meaning therefore transformed, again beyond the control of any author or the notion of authorial intent. Derrida points out that, because the written sign (qua writing) is iterable and can be extracted from any context, its function or meaning cannot be contained by, or reduced to, any finite context; (c) the break with what we call context indicates for Derrida the spacing of which any writing partakes in the first place in order to be meaningful. A written sign, in order to be meaningful, has to function not only through its immediate presence but, importantly, in its spatial **difference** from other signs. The spacing by which meaning emerges and is in fact possible at all is not a simple blank space or 'negative' for Derrida but is, instead, that which makes the mark or inscription possible. In pursuing these aspects of writing by giving attention initially to the written sign, narrowly conceived as the written or printed words on a page, Derrida demonstrates how all language, including spoken language and images, is in fact a writing, available only through spacing, through difference (and more significantly, *différance*). Thus not only is there no immediacy or plenitude in any sign, but writing, far from being the secondary, debased **supplement** to the spoken word and to the idea of language in general (and with that the promise of presence for which the vocable apparently acts as guarantor), is, in fact, that which makes any communication possible, even while, as writing, all signs can only refer to other signs, without ever attaining semantic or syntagmatic stability.

Z

Zeugma—Grammatical and rhetorical term where a single word or phrase, often a predicate, functions in more than one way or refers to two different subjects at the same time.

Areas of Literary, Critical and Cultural Study, with Bibliographies

The following, brief definitions of areas of study and disciplinary focus are not intended to be exhaustive. They serve simply as indications of the principal concerns. Students should refer to works in the bibliographies accompanying each area of interest for key studies of particular disciplines. The bibliographies are selective rather than exhaustive, but are chosen to reflect both recognised exemplary introductions and key influential texts of the areas in question. Furthermore, each area is not of course to be considered exclusive of other literary-theoretical concerns. Readers will note, for example, that feminist studies of literature will be found under 'African-American criticism' and 'ecocriticism', among others. Similarly, there is considerable implicit, if not explicit, overlap between categories such as 'cultural studies', 'marxism', 'cultural materialism', 'new historicism' and 'postmarxism'. Again, as another example, psychoanalytic textual analysis is of interest among feminists, poststructuralists and so on. There is no absolutely justifiable limit to impose upon any aspect of thought or intellectual praxis, other than as a strategic marker of philosophical and polemical identification. At best, the reader should take the categories as provisional rather than rigid or prescriptive, given that the nature of much literary study, inflected by what is called theoretical interests, is marked by hybridity, heterogeneity and protean mutability, as areas of study have developed over time, and as critics have sought to debate and interact with one another, and with the often fraught discursive, ideological and epistemological frameworks from which their work emerges and by which it is articulated.

African-American Criticism

African-American studies finds its modern origins in the Black Arts Movement of the 1960s, which dramatically altered North American attitudes regarding the function and meaning of literature as well as the place of ethnic literature in English departments. The Black Arts Movement established African-American literature as a populist art form, while also spawning publishing houses, theatre troupes and study groups. Often associated with such scholars as Henry Louis Gates, Jr, Cornel West, Deborah McDowell and Houston A. Baker, Jr, among others, African-American Studies seeks to create socio-political awareness for various aspects of interracial tension and the relevance of African history and culture to blacks in the United States.

Bibliography

Andrews, William. *To Tell a Free Story: The First Century of Afro-American Autobiography, 1760–1865*. Urbana, IL, 1986.

Baker, Jr, Houston A. and Patricia Redmond (eds). *Afro-American Literary Study in the 1990s*. Chicago, 1989.

Baker, Jr, Houston A. *Blues, Ideology, and Afro-American Literature*. Chicago, 1984.

Baker, Jr, Houston A. *Black Studies, Rap, and the Academy*. Chicago, 1993.

Baker, Jr, Houston A. *Modernism and the Harlem Renaissance*. Chicago, 1991.

Bambara, Toni Cade (ed.). *The Black Woman: An Anthology*. New York, 1970.

Blassingame, John (ed.). *Slave Testimony: Two Centuries of Letters, Speeches, Interviews, and Autobiographies*. Baton Rouge, LA, 1977.

Carby, Hazel V. *Reconstructing Womanhood: The Emergence of the Afro-American Woman Novelist*. New York, 1987.

Christian, Barbara. *Black Women Novelists: The Development of a Tradition, 1892–1976*. Westport, CT, 1980.

Christian, Barbara. *Black Feminist Criticism*. New York, 1985.

Collins, Patricia Hill. *Black Feminist Thought: Knowledge, Consciousness, and the Politics of Empowerment*. New York, 2000.

Davis, Angela Y. *Women, Race and Class*. New York, 1981.

Douglass, Frederick. *Narrative of the Life of Frederick Douglass, An*

American Slave, Written by Himself, ed. Houston A. Baker. New York, 1982.

Du Bois, W. E. B. *Souls of Black Folk*. New York, 1961.

Ford, Nick Aaron. *Black Studies: Threat or Challenge*. Port Washington, 1973.

Frye, Charles A. *Impact of Black Studies on the Curricula of Three Universities*. Washington, 1976.

Gates, Jr, Henry Louis (ed.). *Black Literature and Literary Theory*. New York, 1984.

Gates, Jr, Henry Louis (ed.). *The Classic Slave Narratives*. New York, 1987.

Gates, Jr, Henry Louis. *The Signifying Monkey: A Theory of African-American Literary Criticism*. New York, 1988.

Gates, Jr, Henry Louis (ed.). *Reading Black, Reading Feminist*. New York, 1990.

Gayle, Addison (ed.). *The Black Aesthetic*. New York, 1971.

Holloway, Karla F. C. *Moorings and Metaphors*. New Brunswick, NJ, 1992.

hooks, bell. *Ain't I a Woman: Black Women and Feminism*. Boston, 1981.

Hull, Gloria T. et al. (eds). *All the Women are White, All the Blacks are Men, But Some of Us are Brave*. Old Westbury, 1982.

Jablon, Madelyn. *Black Metafiction: Self-Consciousness in African-American Literature*. Iowa City, IA, 1997.

Lorde, Audre. *Sister Outsider*. Freedom, 1984.

Smith, Barbara. *The Truth That Never Hurts: Writings on Race, Gender, and Freedom*. New Brunswick, NJ, 1998.

Stepto, Robert and Dexter Fisher (eds). *Afro-American Literature: The Reconstruction of Instruction*. New York, 1978.

Stepto, Robert. *From Behind the Veil: A Study in Afro-American Narrative*. New York, 1979.

Washington, Mary Helen (ed.). *Black-Eyed Susans: Classic Stories By and About Black Women*. New York, 1975.

Washington, Mary Helen. *Invented Lives*. New York, 1987.

Archetypal Criticism

Originating in the work of psychoanalyst Carl Jung, archetypal criticism addresses series of archetypes (myths, patterns, images, figures, symbolic cycles or dreams) in various literary forms. Often appropriated by the proponents of the new criticism during the early part of the twentieth century, archetypal criticism attempts to delineate patterns of plot or character and the ways in which they reveal what Jung refers to as 'racial memory', or the collective memories of the entire human race. Hence, such 'primordial images' impact our shared sense of human experience – our 'collective unconscious', according to Jung. Northrop Frye refined Jung's notion of archetypes in his landmark volume, *The Anatomy of Criticism* (1957), a text that concretised archetypal criticism's place as a primary form of textual practice during the 1960s and 1970s. However, it was Frye's study of Blake, *Fearful Symmetry*, from a decade earlier (1947), which, because of its insistence on matters of overarching, structuring, symbolic patterning in the work of the poet, did much to lay the groundwork for archetypal analysis. Moreover, Frye's work on myth and the Bible has continued to influence scholars.

Bibliography

Bodkin, Maud. *Archetypal Patterns in Poetry*. London, 1934.

Brady, Patrick. *Memory and History as Fiction: An Archetypal Approach to the Historical Novel*. Knoxville, TN, 1993.

Byrnes, Alice. *The Child as Archetypal Symbol in Literature for Children and Adults*. New York, 1995.

Cech, John. *Angels and Wild Things: The Archetypal Poetics of Maurice Sendak*. University Park, PA, 1995.

Doll, Mary Aswell. *Beckett and Myth: An Archetypal Approach*. Syracuse, NY, 1988.

Frye, Northrop. *Fearful Symmetry: A Study of William Blake*. Princeton, NJ, 1947.

Frye, Northrop. *The Anatomy of Criticism: Four Essays*. Princeton, NJ, 1957.

Frye, Northrop. *Fables of Identity: Studies in Poetic Mythology*. New York, 1963.

Frye, Northrop. *Spiritus Mundi: Essays on Literature, Myth, and Society*. Bloomington, IN, 1976.

Frye, Northrop. *The Great Code: The Bible and Literature*. New York, 1982.

Jung, C. G. *The Archetypes and the Collective Unconscious*, trans. R. F. C. Hull. Princeton, NJ, 1969.

Knutson, Harold C. *Molière: An Archetypal Approach*. Toronto, 1976.

Krieger, Murray. *Northrop Frye in Modern Criticism: Selected Papers from the English Institute*. New York, 1966.

Luciano, Patrick. *Them or Us: Archetypal Interpretations of the Fifties Alien Invasion Films*. Bloomington, IN, 1987.

Pratt, Annis. *Archetypal Patterns in Women's Fiction*. Bloomington, IN, 1981.

Schueler, H. J. *The Old Retold: Archetypal Patterns in German Literature of the Nineteenth and Twentieth Centuries*. New York, 1996.

Weiss, Hanna Kalter. *Archetypal Images in Surrealist Prose: A Study in Modern Fiction*. New York, 1988.

Bakhtin and Dialogic Criticism

Dialogic criticism has developed in large part from the work of Russian formalist critic Mikhail M. Bakhtin, whose theories of dialogism and discourse analysis have registered a significant impact upon the nature of contemporary literary and cultural criticism since the translation of his works during the 1980s. In volumes such as *The Dialogic Imagination: Four Essays* (1981), Bakhtin differentiates between monologic, single-voiced works in which a given culture's dominant ideology contradicts subordinate textual voices and dialogic, multivoiced texts that allow numerous voices to emerge and engage in dialogue with one another. In his essay, 'Discourse in the Novel', Bakhtin argues that 'form and content in discourse are one, once we understand that verbal discourse is a social phenomenon – social throughout its entire range and in each and every one of its factors, from the sound image to the furthest reaches of abstract meaning'. Bakhtin's theories of dialogism and *carnival* have not only influenced the direction of reader-response theory in recent decades, but have also participated in the advent of cultural studies and a revival of interest in the analysis of the formal properties of literary works.

Bibliography

Bakhtin, Mikhail. *Rabelais and His World*, trans. Hélène Iswolsky. Cambridge, MA, 1968.

Bakhtin, Mikhail. *The Dialogic Imagination: Four Essays by M.M. Bakhtin*, ed. Michael Holquist, trans. Caryl Emerson and Michael Holquist. Austin, TX, 1981.

Bakhtin, Mikhail. *Problems of Dostoevsky's Poetics*, ed. and trans. Caryl Emerson. Minneapolis, MN, 1984.

Bakhtin, M. M. / Medvedev, P. N. *The Formal Method in Literary Scholarship: A Critical Introduction to Sociological Poetics* (pub. under Medvedev), trans. Albert J. Wehrle. Cambridge, MA, 1985.

Bakhtin, Mikhail. *Speech Genres and Other Late Essays*, eds Caryl Emerson and Michael Holquist, trans. Vern W. McGee. Austin, TX, 1986.

Bakhtin, Mikhail. *Art and Answerability: Early Philosophical Essays by M. M. Bakhtin*, eds Michael Holquist and Vadim Liapunov, trans. Vadim Liapunov. Austin, TX, 1990.

Bauer, Dale, and Susan McKinsky (eds). *Feminism, Bakhtin, and the Dialogic*. Albany, NY, 1991.

Bialostosky, Don H. *Wordsworth, Dialogics, and the Practice of Criticism*. Cambridge, 1992.

Booker, M. Keith. *Joyce, Bakhtin, and the Literary Tradition: Towards a Comparative Cultural Poetics*. Ann Arbor, MI, 1995.

Castle, Terry. *Masquerade and Civilization: The Carnivalesque in Eighteenth-Century Culture and Fiction*. Stanford, CA, 1986.

Clark, Katerina and Michael Holquist. *Mikhail Bakhtin*. Cambridge, MA, 1984.

Emerson, Caryl. *The First Hundred Years of Mikhail Bakhtin*. Princeton, NJ, 1997.

Emerson, Caryl (ed.). *Critical Essays on M. M. Bakhtin*. New York, 1997.

Hirschkop, Ken, and David Shepherd (eds). *Bakhtin and Cultural Theory*. Manchester, 1989.

Holquist, Michael. *Dialogism: Bakhtin and His World*. London, 1990.

Kershner, R. B. *Joyce, Bakhtin, and Popular Literature: Chronicles of Disorder*. Chapel Hill, NC, 1989.

Lodge, David. *After Bakhtin: Essays on Fiction and Criticism*. New York, 1990.

Morris, Pam (ed.) *The Bakhtin Reader: Selected Writings of Bakhtin, Medvedev, Volosinov*. London, 1994.

Morson, Gary Saul (ed.). *Bakhtin: Essays and Dialogues on His Work*. Chicago, 1986.

Morson, Gary Saul and Caryl Emerson (eds.) *Rethinking Bakhtin: Extensions and Challenges*. Evanston, IL, 1989.

Morson, Gary Saul, and Caryl Emerson. *Mikhail Bakhtin: Creation of a Prosaics*. Stanford, CA, 1990.

Sebeok, Thomas A. (ed.). *Carnival!* New York, 1984.

Todorov, Tzvetan. *Mikhail Bakhtin: The Dialogical Principle*, trans. Wlad Godzich. Minneapolis, MN, 1984.

Voloshinov, V. N. *Marxism and the Philosophy of Language*, trans. Ladislav Matejka and I. R. Titunik. Cambridge, MA, 1986.
Voloshinov, V. N. *Freudianism: A Critical Sketch*, eds I. R. Titunik and Neil R. Bruss, trans. I. R. Titunik. Bloomington, IN, 1987.

Chicago School

The Chicago school flourished from the later 1930s into the 1950s, and was centred around the work of Ronald Salmon Crane. Drawing on Aristotle's *Rhetoric* and *Poetics* as their theoretical base texts, the Chicago school believed, along with T. S. Eliot, that criticism should study 'poetry as poetry and not another thing'. They viewed with suspicion what they regarded as new criticism's practice of rejecting historical analysis, its penchant for presenting subjective judgements as objective analysis and its emphasis on poetry rather than other genres such as fiction. Crane and others examined all genres drawing for their techniques on a pluralistic and instrumentalist basis. Many of the publications identified with what is regarded as the Chicago school were produced during the 1930s as part of a ferment created by the radical reorganization of undergraduate education at the University of Chicago. Central to Crane's ideas and crucial for the Chicago school was the notion of *pluralism*. Underlying 'pluralism' is a relativist approach that advocates many different forms of literary criticism, each of which has its own interpretative powers and limitations. The Chicago school, in other words, did not advocate one method, but several, to be adopted pragmatically as dictated by the needs of the given text and situation.

Bibliography

Carey, James. 'The Chicago School and the History of Mass Communication Research', in *James Carey A Critical Reader*, eds Eve Stryker Munson and Catherine A. Warren. Minneapolis, MN, 1997.
Crane, R. S. (ed.) *Critics and Criticism: Ancient and Modern*. Chicago, 1952.
Crane, R. S. *The Languages of Criticism and the Structure of Poetry*. Toronto, 1953.

Crane, R. S. 'The Chicago Critics', in *Princeton Encyclopedia of Poetry and Poetics*, ed. A. Preminger. Princeton, NJ, 1965.

Crane, R. S. *The Idea of the Humanities and Other Essays Critical and Historical*, 2 vols. Chicago, 1967.

Crane, R. S. *Critical and Historical Principles of Literary History*. Chicago, 1971.

Olson, Elder (ed.). *Aristotle's Poetics and English Literature: A Collection of Critical Essays*. Chicago, 1965.

Olson, Elder. *On Value Judgments in the Arts and Other Essays*. Chicago, 1976.

Chicano/Chicana Studies

Chicano/chicana studies finds its roots in a literary movement among Latino writers of the United States that has been gathering momentum since the 1960s. Such writers derive from a variety of Spanish-speaking origins – Mexican, Cuban, Dominican, Puerto Rican, Central and South American – and have been establishing new stylistic and literary practices in order to express their own perspectives of life and culture in the United States. Much of the work of chicano/chicana scholars involves the recovery of the rich culture of literature created by the Hispanic community in the United States since the seventeenth century. Chicano/chicana literature involves a wide variety of stylistic nuances and textual forms, including, for example, a range of oral literary styles from stories and poetry to *dichos* (folk sayings) and *pastorelas* (seasonal plays).

Bibliography

Anzaldúa, Gloria (ed.). *Making Face, Making Soul. Haciendo Caras: Creative and Critical Perspectives by Feminists of Color*. San Francisco, 1990.

Anzaldúa, Gloria. *Borderlands/La Frontera*. San Francisco, 1999.

Arteaga, Alfred. *Chicano Poetics: Heterotexts and Hybridities*. New York, 1997.

Broyles-González, Yolanda. *El Teatro Campesino: Theater in the Chicano Movement*. Austin, TX, 1996.

Castillo, Ana. *Massacre of the Dreamers: Essays on Xicanisma*. Albuquerque, NM, 1994.

García, Alma M. *Chicana Feminist Thought: The Basic Historical Writings*. New York, 1997.
Gaspar de Alba, Alicia. *Chicano Art: Inside/Outside the Master's House*. Texas, 1998.
Gómez-Quiñones, Juan. *Chicano Politics: Reality and Promise 1940–1900*. Albuquerque, NM, 1992.
Gonzales-Berry, Erlinda and Chuck Tatum (eds). *Recovering the U.S. Hispanic Literary Heritage*. Vol. II. Houston, TX, 1996.
Gutiérrez, Ramón, and Genaro Padilla (eds). *Recovering the U.S. Hispanic Literary Heritage*. Houston, TX, 1993.
Hernández-Gutiérrez, Manuel de Jesús, and David William Foster (eds) *Literatura Chicana, 1965–1995: An Anthology in Spanish, English and Caló*. New York, 1997.
Herrera-Sobek, María and Virginia Sánchez Korrol. *Recovering the U.S. Hispanic Literary Heritage*, Vol. III. Houston, TX, 2000.
Herrera-Sobek, María and Helena María Viramontes. *Chicana Creativity and Criticism: New Frontiers in American Literature*. Albuquerque, NM, 1996.
Isasi-Díaz, Ada María. *En la Lucha/In the Struggle: A Hispanic Woman's Liberation Theology*. Minneapolis, MN, 1993.
López, Tiffany Ana. *Growing Up Chicana/o*. New York, 1993.
Mariscal, George (ed.). *Aztlán and Viet Nam: Chicano and Chicana Experiences of the War*. Berkeley, CA, 1999.
Martínez, Julio A. and Francisco A. Lomelí (eds). *Chicano Literature: A Reference Guide*. Connecticut, 1985.
Moraga, Cherríe, *Loving in the War Years: lo que nunca pasó por sus labios*. Boston, 1983.
Moraga, Cherríe and Gloria Anzaldúa. *This Bridge Called My Back: Writings by Radical Women of Color*. New York, 1983.
Pérez, Emma, *The Decolonial Imaginary: Writing Chicanas into History*. Indianapolis, IN, 1999.
Pérez-Torres, Rafael. *Movements in Chicano Poetry: Against Myths, Against Margins*. New York, 1995.
Rebolledo, Tey Diana. *Women Singing in the Snow: A Cultural Analysis of Chicana Literature*. Tucson, AZ, 1995.
Rebolledo, Tey Diana and Eliana S. Rivero (eds). *Infinite Divisions: An Anthology of Chicana Literature*. Tucson, AZ, 1993.
Sánchez, George J. *Becoming Mexican American: Ethnicity, Culture and Identity in Chicano Los Angeles, 1900–1945*. New York, 1993.
Trujillo, Carla. *Living Chicana Theory*. Berkeley, CA, 1998.

Cultural Materialism

Cultural materialism can be defined as an approach to literature and culture which sees literary texts as the material products of specific historical and political conditions, whether one speaks of the moment of production – the plays of Shakespeare as mediations of late sixteenth-century epistemologies and ideologies – or the reception of the text in particular periods – such as the teaching of Shakespeare in high schools today. In examining the relation of the literary to history, in which historical concerns are read not merely as the background or context of the text but as being encoded in particular ways through the textual interests and discourses, cultural materialism shows how meaning is not timeless but the differentiated product of different ideological and discursive formations, as well as of different times, locations and epistemologies. Cultural materialist analysis has often stressed the political functions of literary texts in our own time and, with particular focus on Shakespeare, the conservative appropriation of the playwright in the names of tradition and heritage. In doing so, cultural materialism produces analyses in which the fractures within conservative ideology are exposed, and the subversion of authority is made available.

Bibliography

Barker, Francis. *The Tremulous Private Body: Essays on Subjection.* London, 1984.

Belsey, Catherine. *The Subject of Tragedy: Identity and Difference in Renaissance Drama.* London, 1985.

Brannigan, John. *New Historcism and Cultural Materialism.* Basingstoke, 1998.

Dollimore, Jonathan. *Radical Tragedy: Religion, Ideology and Power in the Drama of Shakespeare and his Contemporaries.* Hemel Hempstead, 1984.

Dollimore, Jonathan. *Sexual Dissidence: Augustine to Wilde, Freud to Foucault.* Oxford, 1991.

Dollimore, Jonathan, and Alan Sinfield (eds). *Political Shakespeare: New Essays in Cultural Materialism.* Manchester, 1985.

Drakakis, John (ed.). *Alternative Shakespeares.* London, 1985.

Hawkes, Terence (ed.). *Alternative Shakespeares Volume 2*. London, 1996.

Hawthorn, Jeremy. *Cunning Passages: New Historcism, Cultural Materialism and Marxism in the Contemporary Literary Debate*. London, 1996.

Holderness, Graham (ed.). *The Shakespeare Myth*. Manchester, 1988.

Milner, Andrew. *Cultural Materialism*. Carlton, 1993.

Prendergast, Christopher (ed.). *Cultural Materialism: On Raymond Williams*. Minneapolis, MN, 1995.

Ryan, Kiernan (ed.). *New Historcism and Cultural Materialism: A Reader*. London, 1996.

Sinfield, Alan. *Literature in Protestant England 1560–1660*. London, 1982.

Sinfield, Alan (ed.). *Society and Literature 1945–1970*. London, 1983.

Sinfield, Alan. *Alfred Tennyson*. Oxford, 1986.

Sinfield, Alan. *Literature, Politics and Culture in Postwar Britain*. Oxford, 1989.

Sinfield, Alan. *Faultlines: Cultural Materialism and the Politics of Dissident Reading*. Oxford, 1992.

Sinfield, Alan. *Cultural Politics – Queer Reading*. London, 1994.

Sinfield, Alan. *The Wilde Century: Effeminacy, Oscar Wilde and the Queer Moment*. London, 1994.

Wilson, Scott. *Cultural Materialism: Theory and Practice*. Oxford, 1995.

Cultural Studies

Cultural studies finds its origins in the British cultural studies movement of the late 1950s and early 1960s, particularly via the publication of influential works by Richard Hoggart and Raymond Williams. In 1964, Hoggart and Stuart Hall founded Birmingham University's Centre for Contemporary Cultural Studies, an institution that soon became synonymous with the cultural studies movement of that era. Attempting to respond to the many facets of mass culture intrinsic to postwar British life, such theorists devoted initial attention to postwar shifts in the lives of working-class Britons confronted with the changes inherent in modernisation, as well as with the disintegration of traditional familial roles and social practices. Later manifestations of culture studies, particularly in the United States, critiqued the radical consequences of making distinctions between conventional notions of 'culture' and 'society', and between 'high culture' and 'low culture'. Culture studies' development in the latter decades of the twentieth century is characterised by its intersection with a variety of disciplines and political forms of literary criticism, from deconstruction and postmodernism to gender studies and environmental criticism.

Bibliography

Arnold, Matthew. *Culture and Anarchy*. Cambridge, 1966.

Brantlinger, Patrick. *Crusoe's Footprints: Cultural Studies in Britain and America*. London, 1990.

Centre for Contemporary Cultural Studies, University of Birmingham. *The Empire Strikes Back: Race and Racism in 70's Britain*. London, 1982.

Collins, Richard et al. (eds). *Media, Culture and Society: A Critical Reader*. London, 1986.

Davies, Ioan. *Cultural Studies and Beyond: Fragments of Empire*. London, 1995.

Dworkin, Dennis. *Cultural Marxism in Postwar Britain: History, The New Left, and the Origins of Cultural Studies*. Durham, 1997.

Easthope, Antony. *Literary into Cultural Studies*. London, 1991.

Fiske, John and John Hartley. *Reading Television*. London, 1978.

Franklin, Sarah, Celia Lury and Jackie Stacy (eds). *Off Center: Feminism and Cultural Studies*. New York, 1991.

Gilroy, Paul. *There Ain't No Black in the Union Jack*. London, 1987.

Gilroy, Paul. *The Black Atlantic: Modernity and Double Consciousness*. Cambridge, MA, 1993.

Grossberg, Lawrence, Cary Nelson and Paula Treichler (eds). *Cultural Studies*. New York, 1992.

Hall, Stuart. *The Hard Road to Renewal: Thatcherism and the Crisis of the Left*. London, 1988.

Hall, Stuart and Paul du Gay (eds). *Questions of Cultural Identity*. London, 1996.

Hall, Stuart and Martin Jacques (eds). *The Politics of Thatcherism*. London, 1983.

Hall, Stuart and Martin Jacques (eds). *New Times: The Changing Face of Politics in the 1990s*. London, 1989.

Hall, Stuart and Tony Jefferson (eds). *Resistance Through Rituals: Youth Subcultures in Postwar Britain*. London, 1976.

Hall, Stuart and Paddy Whannel. *The Popular Arts*. London, 1964.

Hall, Stuart et al. (eds). *Policing the Crisis: Mugging, the State, and Law and Order.* London, 1978.

Hall, Stuart et al. (eds). *Culture, Media, Language: Working Papers in Cultural Studies, 1972–79.* London, 1980.

Hall, Stuart et al. (eds). *State and Society in Contemporary Britain: A Critical Introduction.* Cambridge, 1984.

Hebdige, Dick. *Subculture: The Meaning of Style.* London, 1979.

Hewison, Robert. *Culture and Consensus: England, Art and Politics since 1940.* London, 1994.

Hoggart, Richard. *The Uses of Literacy.* Harmondsworth, 1992.

Inglis, Fred. *Cultural Studies.* Oxford, 1993.

Mercer, Kobena. *Welcome to the Jungle: New Positions in Black Cultural Studies.* London, 1994.

Milner, Andrew. *Cultural Materialism.* Melbourne, 1993.

Morley, David, and Kuan-Hsing Chen (eds). *Stuart Hall: Critical Dialogues in Cultural Studies.* London, 1996.

Munns, Jessica and Gita Rajan (eds). *A Cultural Studies Reader: History, Theory, Practice.* London, 1995.

Nelson, Cary and Dillip Goankar (eds). *Disciplinarity and Dissent in Cultural Studies.* New York, 1996.

O'Connor, Alan. *Raymond Williams: Writing, Culture, Politics.* Oxford, 1989.

Sardar, Ziauddin and Borin Van Woon. *Introducing Cultural Studies.* New York, 1998.

Sarup, Madan. *Identity, Culture, and the Postmodern World.* Athens, OH, 1996.

Sinfield, Alan. *Cultural Politics—Queer Reading.* London, 1994.

Storey, John. *An Introductory Guide to Cultural Theory and Popular Culture.* Athens, OH, 1993.

Storey, John (ed.). *Cultural Theory and Popular Culture: A Reader.* Hemel Hempstead, 1994.

Storey, John (ed.). *What is Cultural Studies?* London, 1996.

Thompson, E. P. *The Making of the English Working Class.* London, 1963.

Turner, Graeme. *British Cultural Studies: An Introduction,* 2nd edn. London, 1996.

Williams, Raymond. *Culture and Society 1780–1950.* London, 1958.

Williams, Raymond. *The Long Revolution.* London, 1961.

Williams, Raymond. *Communications.* Harmondsworth, 1962.

Williams, Raymond. *Television: Technology and Cultural Form.* New York, 1975.

Williams, Raymond. *Marxism and Literature.* Oxford, 1977.

Williams, Raymond. *Problems in Materialism and Culture: Selected Essays*. London, 1980.

Williams, Raymond. *Towards 2000*. London, 1983.

Williams, Raymond. *Resources of Hope*. London, 1989.

Williamson, Judith. *Decoding Advertisements: Ideology and Meaning in Advertising*. London, 1978.

Wolin, Richard. *The Terms of Cultural Criticism: The Frankfurt School, Existentialism, Poststructuralism*. New York, 1992.

Women's Studies Group, Centre for Contemporary Cultural Studies, University of Birmingham. *Women Take Issue: Aspects of Women's Subordination*. London, 1978.

Discourse Analysis

Discourse analysis emerged in the 1970s, when critical and cultural theorists explored the manner in which language performs contextual and situational functions in the act of running, or ongoing, discourse. Discourse analysis examines the interrelationship between the speaker (or writer) and the auditor (or reader) in a given context with its attendant social and cultural conventions. Discourse analysis is associated with a number of theorists, including Hans Georg Gadamer, Michel Foucault and Clifford Geertz, among others. Of particular significance is the concept of *implicature*, which was coined in 1975 by speech-act philosopher H. P. Grice. Implicature refers to the inherent indirection in spoken discourse. Grice contends that we use such statements as means for sharing a series of what he describes as 'communicative presumptions'. Contemporary discourse analysts discuss the roles of dialogue, stylistics and point of view in conversation and language.

Bibliography

Austin, J. L. *How To Do Things With Words*. Oxford, 1962.

Bakhtin, Mikhail M. *Speech Genres and Other Late Essays*, 1953. Austin, TX, 1986.

Bazerman, Charles. *Shaping Written Knowledge*. Madison, WI, 1988.

Bernstein, Basil B. *Class, Codes, and Control*, 2 vols. London, 1971, 1975.

Brazil, David, Malcolm Coulthard and Catherine Johns. *Discourse Intonation and Language Teaching*. London, 1980.

Brown, Gillian and George Yule. *Discourse Analysis*. Cambridge, 1983.

Cazden, Courtney B. *Classroom Discourse: The Language of Teaching and Learning*. Portsmouth, 1988.

Coulthard, Malcolm. *Introduction to Discourse Analysis*. London, 1977.

Gee, J. P. *Social Linguistics and Literacies*. London, 1990.

Gregory, Michael, and Susanne Carroll. *Language and Situation: Language Varieties and Their Social Contexts*. London, 1978.

Halliday, M. A. K. *Language as Social Semiotic*. London, 1978.

Halliday, M. A. K. *An Introduction to Functional Grammar*. London, 1985.

Halliday, M. A. K., and Ruqaiya Hasan. *Language, Context, and Text*. Oxford, 1989.

Hoey, Michael. *Textual Interaction: an Introduction to Written Discourse Analysis*. London, 2000.

Hunston, Susan and Geoff Thompson (eds). *Evaluation in Text: Authorial Stance and the Construction of Discourse*. Oxford, 2000.

Kendon, Adam. *Conducting Interaction*. Cambridge, 1990.

Lave, Jean. *Cognition in Practice*. Cambridge, 1988.

Martin, J. R. *Factual Writing: Exploring and Challenging Social Reality*. Oxford, 1989.

Meyer, Michael. *Methods of Text and Discourse Analysis*. London, 2000.

Porter, Stanley E. *Discourse Analysis and the New Testament: Approaches and Results*. Sheffield, 1999.

Sinclair, John and Malcolm Coulthard. *Towards an Analysis of Discourse*. Oxford, 1975.

Stubbs, Michael. *Language and Literacy: The Sociolinguistics of Reading and Writing*. London, 1980.

Stubbs, Michael. *Discourse Analysis: The Sociolinguistic Analysis of Natural Language*. Chicago, 1983.

Swales, J. *Genre Analysis*. Cambridge, MN, 1991.

Thibault, Paul J. *Social Semiotics as Praxis*. Minneapolis, 1991.

Thibault, Paul J. *Re-reading Saussure: The Dynamics of Signs in Social Life*. London, 1997.

Ecocriticism

Ecocriticism names that area of literary and cultural studies which studies the relationship between human culture and society and the natural world. The earliest work in ecocriticism sought to reread canonical texts with a view to consideration of textual explorations and representations of the natural world. In particular, ecocritics addressed and analysed romanticism's textual debt to the idea of nature. Subsequently, after the initial critical engagement, ecocriticism in the last decade has attempted to expand the canon through a rereading of 'nature writing', typified, on the one hand, by Thoreau's publications and, on the other, the work of Native American writers. In the analysis of the representation and construction of nature in the text, ecocritics have also turned to matters of gender and race in their relationship to the discursive mediation of the natural environment, while, at the same time, reading the 'natural world' in the text as the articulation of a non-human other.

Bibliography

Adamson, Joni. *American Indian Literature, Environmental Justice, and Ecocriticism: The Middle Place*. Tucson, AZ, 2001.

Association for the Study of Literature and Environment. ASLE Online http//:www.asle.umn.edu

Bate, Jonathan. *Romantic Ecology: Wordsworth and the Environmental Tradition*. London, 1991.

Bate, Jonathan. *The Song of the Earth*. London, 2000.

Bennett, Michael, and David W. Teague (eds). *The Nature of Cities: Ecocriticism and Urban Environments*. Tucson, AZ, 1999.

Bleakley, Alan. *The Animalizing Imagination: Totemism, Textuality, and Ecocriticism*. Basingstoke, 2000.

Cooley, John R. (ed.). *Earthly Words: Essays on Contemporary American Nature and Environmental Writers*. Ann Arbor, MI, 1994.

Coupe, Laurence (ed.). *The Green Studies Reader: From Romanticism to Ecocriticism*. New York, 2000.

Elgin, Don D. *The Comedy of the Fantastic: Ecological Perspectives on the Fantasy Novel*. Westport, CT, 1985.

Gaard, Greta and Patrick D. Murphy (eds). *Ecofeminist Literary Criticism: Theory, Interpretation, Pedagogy*. Urbana, IL, 1998.

Glotfelty, Cheryl and Harold Fromm (eds). *The Ecocriticism Reader: Landmarks and Literary Ecology*. Athens, OH, 1996.

Kerridge, Richard and Neil Sammels (ed.). *Writing the Environment: Ecocriticism and Literature*. London, 1998.

Kroeber, Karl. *Ecological Literary Criticism: Romantic Imagining and the Biology of the Mind.* New York, 1994.

Mazel, David. *American Literary Environmentalism.* Athens, OH, 2000.

Murphy, Patrick D. *Farther Afield in the Study of Nature-Oriented Literature.* Charlottesville, VA, 2000.

Nelson, Barney. *The Wild and the Domestic: Animal Representation, Ecocriticism, and Western American Literature.* Reno, NV, 2000.

Tallmadge, John, and Henry Harrington (eds). *Reading Under the Sign of Nature: New Essays in Ecocriticism.* Salt Lake City, UT, 2000.

Tichi, Cecelia. *New World, New Earth: Environmental Reform in American Literature from Puritans Through Whitman.* New Haven, CT, 1979.

Voros, Gyorgyi. *Notation of the Wild: Ecology in the Poetry of Wallace Stevens.* Iowa City, IA, 1997.

Waage, Frederick O. (ed.). *Teaching Environmental Literature: Materials, Methods, Resources.* New York, 1985.

Ethical Criticism

Ethical criticism's emergence as an interpretative paradigm finds its origins in the latter half of the twentieth century and is often associated with such figures as F. R. Leavis, John Gardner, Wayne C. Booth, Martha C. Nussbaum and J. Hillis Miller, among others. In scholarly circles, ethical criticism in literary studies functions both as a response to the poststructuralist theoretical concerns of deconstruction and postmodernism as well as to the growing scholarly interest in the humanistic interpretation of literary works. The emergence of such critical movements as gender studies, historical criticism and culture studies accounts for the revival of ethical criticism, which explores the nature of ethical issues and their roles in the creation and interpretation of literary works. The recent apotheosis of ethical criticism finds its origins in the North American academy – and particularly as a result of the institutionalisation of English studies and literary theory in the United States. In European circles, ethical criticism has taken on entirely different theoretical dimensions and is often associated with the philosophy of Emmanuel Levinas. There has, moreover, been what has been perceived as an 'ethical turn' in the work of those associated with deconstruction, particularly the work of Jacques Derrida (whose work is, in part, influenced by and a response to Levinas), though, arguably, the ethical dimension has always been at work.

Bibliography

Booth, Wayne C. *The Company We Keep: An Ethics of Fiction*. Berkeley, CA, 1988.

Champagne, Roland. *The Ethics of Reading According to Emmanuel Levinas*. Amsterdam, 1998.

Chanter, Tina. *Ethics of Eros: Irigaray's Rewriting of the Philosophers*. London, 1995.

Clausen, Christopher. *The Moral Imagination: Essays on Literature and Ethics*. Iowa City, IA, 1986.

Cornell, Drucilla. *Beyond Accommodation: Ethical Feminism, Deconstruction, and the Law*. Lanham, MA, 1999.

Critchley, Simon. *Very Little Almost Nothing: Death, Philosophy, Literature*. London, 1997.

Critchley, Simon. *The Ethics of Deconstruction: Derrida and Levinas*, 2nd edn. West Lafayette, IN, 1999.

Critchley, Simon. *Ethics–Politics–Subjectivity*. London, 1999.

Davis, Todd F., and Kenneth Womack (eds). *Mapping the Ethical Turn: Ethics and Literature in New Theoretical Contexts*. Charlottesville, 2001.

Eaglestone, Robert. *Ethical Criticism: Reading after Levinas*. Edinburgh, 1997.

Garber, Marjorie, Beatrice Hanssen and Rebecca L. Walkowitz (eds). *The Turn to Ethics*. London, 2000.

Gardner, John. *On Moral Fiction*. New York, 1978.

Gatens, Moira. *Imaginary Bodies: Ethics, Power and Corporeality*. London, 1996.

Gibson, Andrew. *Postmodernity, Ethics, and the Novel: From Leavis to Levinas*. London, 1999.

Goldberg, S. L. *Agents and Lives: Moral Thinking in Literature*. Cambridge, 1993.

Graff, Gerald. *Literature against Itself: Literary Ideas in Modern Society*. Chicago, 1979.

Harpham, Geoffrey Galt. *Getting It Right: Language, Literature, and Ethics*. Chicago, 1992.

Harpham, Geoffrey Galt. *Shadows of Ethics: Criticism and the Just Society*. Durham, NC, 1999.

Irigaray, Luce. *An Ethics of Sexual Difference*, trans. Carolyn Burke and Gillian C. Gill. Ithaca, NY, 1993.

Levinas, Emmanuel. *Basic Philosophical Writings*, eds Adriaan T. Pe-
perzak, Simon Critchley, and Robert Bernasconi. Bloomington, IN,
1996.
Miller, J. Hillis. *The Ethics of Reading: Kant, de Man, Eliot, Trollope,
James, and Benjamin*. New York, 1987.
Newton, Adam Zachary. *Narrative Ethics*. Cambridge, MA, 1995.
Norris, Christopher. *Truth and the Ethics of Criticism*. New York,
1994.
Nussbaum, Martha C. *Love's Knowledge: Essays on Philosophy and
Literature*. New York, 1990.
Nussbaum, Martha C. *Poetic Justice: The Literary Imagination and
Public Life*. Boston, 1995.
Nussbaum, Martha C. *The Fragility of Goodness: Luck and Ethics in
Greek Tragedy and Philosophy*. Cambridge, 1986.
Parker, David. *Ethics, Theory, and the Novel*. Cambridge, 1994.
Parr, Susan Resneck. *The Moral of the Story: Literature, Values, and
American Education*. New York, 1982.
Phelan, James (ed.). *Reading Narrative: Form, Ethics, Ideology*. Colum-
bus, 1988.
Robbins, Jill. *Altered Reading: Levinas and Literature*. Chicago, 1999.
Rosenblatt, Louise M. *The Reader, the Text, the Poem: The Transac-
tional Theory of the Literary Work*. Carbondale, IL, 1978.
Siebers, Tobin. *The Ethics of Criticism*. Ithaca, NY, 1988.
Williams, Bernard. *Ethics and the Limits of Philosophy*. Cambridge,
1985.
Worthington, Kim L. *Self as Narrative: Subjectivity and Community in
Contemporary Fiction*. Oxford, 1996.

Feminism

Though not a unified, single critical 'voice', feminist literary
criticisms are in broad agreement on their shared role as political
and politicised criticisms directed at matters of gender, sexuality
and identity. Developing critical languages from the political
discourses of the women's movement of the 1950s and 1960s,
feminist criticism addresses the representation of women in
literature and culture, in the work of both female and male
authors. Critical feminisms have also concerned themselves with
the role of the reader from a gendered perspective and with the
study of women's writing. Feminist criticism has also addressed
the relation of gender to matters of class and race, and has,

furthermore, expanded the canon of literature through the recovery of neglected works by women.

Bibliography

Assiter, Alison. *Enlightened Women: Modernist Feminism in a Postmodern Age.* London, 1996.

Barrett, Michèle. *Women's Oppression Today. The Marxist/Feminist Encounter.* London, 1988.

Barrett, Michèle and Phillips, Anne (eds). *Destabilizing Theory: Contemporary Feminist Debates.* Cambridge, 1992.

Battersby, Christine. *The Phenomenal Woman: Feminist Metaphysics and the Patterns of Identity.* Cambridge, 1998.

Benhabib, Seyla. *Situating the Self: Gender, Community and Postmodernism in Contemporary Ethics.* Cambridge, 1992.

Benhabib, Seyla, Judith Butler, Drucilla Cornell and Nancy Fraser. *Feminist Contentions: A Philosophical Exchange.* New York, 1995.

Bock, Gisela and James, Susan (eds). *Beyond Equality and Difference: Citizenship, Feminist Politics and Female Subjectivity.* London, 1992.

Brennan, Teresa (ed.). *Between Feminism and Psychoanalysis.* London, 1989.

Brown, Wendy. 'The Impossibility of Women's Studies', *differences: A Journal of Feminist and Cultural Studies,* 9, 3 (1997).

Bryson, Valerie. *Feminist Political Theory: An Introduction.* London, 1992.

Butler, Judith. *Gender Trouble: Feminism and the Subversion of Identity.* 10th anniversary edn. New York, 1999.

Caine, Barbara. *English Feminism 1780–1980.* Oxford, 1997.

Cixous, Hélène. *The Hélène Cixous Reader,* foreword Jacques Derrida, ed. Susan Sellers. London, 1994.

Cixous, Hélène, and Catherine Clément. *The Newly Born Woman,* trans. Betsy Wing, intro. Sandra Gilbert. Minneapolis, MN, 1975.

Cornillon, Susan Koppelman. *Images of Women in Fiction: Feminist Perspectives.* Bowling Green, KY, 1972.

Coward, Rosalind. *Female Desire.* London, 1984.

de Beauvoir, Simone. *The Second Sex.* Harmondsworth, 1983.

Eagleton, Mary (ed.). *Feminist Literary Theory,* 2nd edn. Oxford, 1996.

Elam, Diane. *Feminism and Deconstruction: Ms. en Abyme.* New York, 1994.

Elam, Diane, and Robyn Wiegman (eds). *Feminism Beside Itself.* New York, 1995.

Ellmann, Mary. *Thinking About Women.* New York, 1968.

Evans, Judith. *Feminist Theory Today: An Introduction to Second-Wave Feminism*. London, 1995.

Felski, Rita. *Beyond Feminist Aesthetics: Feminist Literature and Social Change*. London, 1989.

Friedan, Betty. *The Feminine Mystique*. Harmondsworth, 1992.

Fuss, Diana. *Essentially Speaking: Feminism, Nature, and Difference*. New York, 1989.

Fuss, Diana (ed.). *Inside/Out: Lesbian Theories, Gay Theories*. New York, 1991.

Gallop, Jane. *Around 1981: Academic Feminist Literary Theory*. New York, 1992.

Garry, Ann and Marilyn Pearsall (eds). *Women, Knowledge and Reality: Explorations in Feminist Philosophy*. London, 1989.

Gatens, Moira. *Imaginary Bodies: Ethics, Power and Corporeality*. London, 1996.

Gilbert, Sandra M. and Susan Gubar. *The Madwoman in the Attic: The Place of the Woman Writer in the Nineteenth-Century Literary Imagination*. New Haven, CT, 1979.

Grosz, Elizabeth and Elspeth Probyn (eds). *Sexy Bodies: The Strange Carnalities of Feminism*. London, 1995.

Gubar, Susan. *Critical Condition: Feminism at the Turn of the Century*. New York, 2000.

Hennessy, Rosemary. *Materialist Feminism and the Politics of Discourse*. New York, 1993.

Hirsch, Marianne and Evelyn Fox Keller (eds). *Conflicts in Feminism*. New York, 1990.

hooks, bel. *Ain't I a Woman? Black Women and Feminism*. London, 1982.

Irigaray, Luce. *Speculum of the Other Woman*, trans. Gillian C. Gill. Ithaca, NY, 1974.

Irigaray, Luce. *This Sex Which Is Not One*, trans. Catherine C. Porter. Ithaca, NY, 1985.

Irigaray, Luce. *The Irigaray Reader*, ed. Margaret Whitford. Oxford, 1991.

Irigaray, Luce. *An Ethics of Sexual Difference*, trans. Carolyn Burke and Gillian C. Gill. Ithaca, NY, 1993.

Johnson, Barbara. *The Feminist Difference: Literature, Psychoanalysis, Race, and Gender*. Cambridge, 1998.

Kemp, Sandra and Judith Squires (eds). *Feminisms*. Oxford, 1997.

Kristeva, Julia. *The Kristeva Reader*, ed. Toril Moi. New York, 1986.

Looser, Devoney and E. Ann Kaplan. *Generations: Academic Feminists in Dialogue*. Minneapolis, MN, 1997.

Lovell, Terry (ed.). *British Feminist Thought: A Reader*. Oxford, 1990.

Lovenduski, Joni and Vicky Randall. *Contemporary Feminist Politics: Women and Power in Britain*. Oxford, 1993.

Mcnay, Lois. *Foucault and Feminism: Power, Gender and the Self*. Cambridge, 1992.

Millett, Kate. *Sexual Politics*. London, 1977.

Mitchell, Juliet. *Woman's Estate*. Harmondsworth, 1971.

Mitchell, Juliet. *Psychoanalysis and Feminism*. London, 1974.

Mitchell, Juliet, and Ann Oakley (eds). *What is Feminism?* Oxford, 1986.

Moers, Ellen. *Literary Women: The Great Writers* [1976]. Oxford, 1985.

Moi, Toril. *Sexual/Textual Politics: Feminist Literary Theory*. New York, 1985.

Nicholson, Linda. *Feminism/Postmodernism*. New York, 1990.

Nicholson, Linda (ed.). *The Second Wave: A Reader in Feminist Theory*. London, 1997.

Riley, Denise. *'Am I That Name?': Feminism and the Category of 'Women' in History*. Basingstoke, 1988.

Robbins, Ruth. *Literary Feminisms*. Basingstoke, 2000.

Rose, Jacqueline. *Sexuality in the Field of Vision*. London, 1986.

Rowbotham, Sheila. *The Past is Before Us*. Harmondsworth, 1990.

Scott, Joan. *Gender and the Politics of History*. New York, 1988.

Shildrick, Margerit. *Leaky Bodies and Boundaries: Feminism, Postmodernism and (Bio)ethics*. London, 1997.

Showalter, Elaine. *A Literature of Their Own: British Women Novelists from Brontë to Lessing*. London, 1978.

Showalter, Elaine (ed.). *The New Feminist Criticism: Essays on Women, Literature and Theory*. London, 1986.

Showalter, Elaine. *The Female Malady: Women, Madness, and English Culture 1830–1980*. New York, 1987.

Smith, Paul and Alice Jardine (eds). *Men in Feminism*. New York, 1987.

Soper, Kate. *Troubled Pleasures: Writings on Politics, Gender and Hedonism*. London, 1990.

Spacks, Patricia Meyer. *The Female Imagination: A Literary and Psychological Investigation of Women's Writing*. London, 1976.

Stanley, Liz. *Feminist Praxis: Research, Theory and Epistemology in Feminist Sociology*. London, 1990.

Todd, Janet. *Feminist Literary History: A Defence*. Cambridge, 1988.

Tong, Rosemary. *Feminist Thought: A Comprehensive Introduction*. Sydney, 1989.

Walby, Sylvia. *Theorizing Patriarchy*. Oxford, 1990.

Waugh, Patricia. *Feminine Fictions: Revisiting the Postmodern*. London, 1989.

Weedon, Chris. *Feminist Practice and Poststructuralist Theory*. Oxford, 1987.

Whelehen, Imelda. *Modern Feminist Thought: From Second Wave to Post-Feminism*. Edinburgh, 1995.

Woolf, Virginia. *A Room of One's Own*. London, 1929.

Frankfurt School

Founded in 1924, The *Institut für Sozialforschung* (Institute for Social Research) of Frankfurt University focused on the historical socialist and labour movements, economic history and the history of political economy through a marxist lens. It is principally with the work of Max Horkheimer, Theodor Adorno, Herbert Marcuse and Jürgen Habermas as expressions of a materialist philosophy (thought being the product of historical conditions), that the Frankfurt school is associated, and which has proved most influential beyond the immediate context of the Frankfurt school's inception and research. In addition to the influence of Marx and post-Hegelian leftist thinking, the text of Nietzsche left its mark, as did the sociology of Max Weber. As the second director of the Institute, Horkheimer sought to retain certain aspects of Hegelian thought while abandoning its idealism, the corrective for which was to be found in Marx's own work in terms of dialectical logic for the consideration of social reality. Adorno's work is marked by an effort to think the history of philosophy alongside the history of consciousness, in materialist terms through sociology as the basis of a critical hermeneutics, cultural and intellectual objects articulating, in mediated fashion, the existing modes of production in society. Marcuse's work is more explicitly marxist in its orientation that that of Horkheimer and Adorno. His publications include analyses of German fascism and the stages of capitalist development, a study of Soviet Marxism, and an attempted synthesis of Freud and Marx. Habermas, the principal figure of the second generation of the Frankfurt school, in his work manifests significant departures from the interests of the first generation, particularly visible in his interests in speech-act theory, a post-Kantian engagement with the reconstruction of the theory of rationality and an open engagement with Anglo-American philosophy.

Bibliography

Adorno, Theodor W. *Prisms*, trans. Samuel and Shierry Weber. London, 1967.

Adorno, Theodor W. *Aesthetic Theory*, trans. Robert Hullot-Kentor. Minneapolis, MN, 1970.

Adorno, Theodor W. *Negative Dialectics*, trans. E. B. Ashton. London, 1973.

Adorno, Theodor W. *Minima Moralia: Reflections on Damaged Life*, trans. E. F. N. Jephcott. London, 1974.

Arato, Andrew and Gebhardt, Eike (eds). *The Essential Frankfurt School Reader*. Oxford, 1978.

Habermas, Jürgen. *Knowledge and Human Interests*, trans. Jeremy J. Shapiro. Boston, 1971.

Habermas, Jürgen. *Theory of Communicative Action. Volume One. Reason and the Rationalization of Society*, trans. Thomas McCarthy. Boston, 1984.

Held, David. 1980. *Introduction to Critical Theory: Horkheimer to Habermas*. London, 1980.

Horkheimer, Max. *Critical Theory: Selected Essays*, trans. Matthew J. O'Connell. New York, 1986.

Horkheimer, Max and Adorno, T.W. *Dialectic of Enlightenment*, trans. John Cumming. London, 1979.

Jay, Martin. *The Dialectical Imagination: A History of the Frankfurt School 1923–50*. London, 1973.

Marcuse, Herbert. *Eros and Civilisation: A Philosophical Inquiry into Freud*. Boston, 1955.

Marcuse, Herbert. *Negations: Essays in Critical Theory*, trans. Jeremy J. Shapiro. Boston, 1968.

Marcuse, Herbert. *One Dimensional Man*, trans. Jeremy J. Shapiro. London, 1968.

Marcuse, Herbert. *Five Lectures: Psychoanalysis, Politics, and Utopia*, trans. Jeremy J. Shapiro and Shierry M. Weber. Boston, 1970.

Marcuse, Herbert. *The Aesthetic Dimension: Toward a Critique of Marxist Aesthetics*. Boston, 1979.

Wiggershaus, Rolf. *The Frankfurt School: Its History, Theories, and Political Significance*, trans. Michael Robertson. Cambridge, MA, 1994.

Gay and Lesbian Studies and Queer Theory

Gay and lesbian studies and queer theory as political and theoretical movements in academic circles have been influenced by the work of such thinkers as Eve Kosofsky Sedgwick, Jonathan Dollimore, Judith Butler and Alan Sinfield, among others. Many theorists locate the origins of the contemporary gay and lesbian studies movement – and hence the emergence of queer theory – in the writings of Oscar Wilde and Michel Foucault. Wilde's status as an icon of homosexuality and Foucault's intellectual theorising of sexuality shared in the construction of twentieth-century value systems and in the creation of transcultural models of homosexuality. Gay studies as a social, intellectual and cultural paradigm finds its origins in the material culture of the 1970s, when the subjective politics of categorisation began to assume ideological proportions.

Bibliography

Abelove, Henry et al. (eds). *The Lesbian and Gay Studies Reader*. New York, 1993.

Bartlett, Neil. *Who Was That Man: A Present for Mr. Oscar Wilde*. London, 1988.

Berlant, Lauren. *The Queen of America Goes to Washington City: Essays on Sex and Citizenship*. Durham, NC, 1997.

Boone, Joseph A. and Michael Cadden (eds). *Engendering Men: The Question of Male Feminist Criticism*. New York, 1990.

Boswell, John. *Christianity, Social Tolerance, and Homosexuality: Gay People in Western Europe from the Beginning of the Christian Era to the Fourteenth Century*. Chicago, 1980.

Bray, Alan. *Homosexuality in Renaissance England*. London, 1982.

Bristow, Joseph. *Sexual Sameness: Textual Differences in Lesbian and Gay Writing*. London, 1992.

Bristow, Joseph. *Effeminate England: Homoerotic Writing After 1885*. New York, 1995.

Butler, Judith. *Gender Trouble: Feminism and the Subversion of Identity*. New York, 1990.

Butler, Judith. *Bodies that Matter: On the Discursive Limits of 'Sex'*. New York, 1993.

Case, Sue-Ellen (ed.) *Performing Feminisms: Feminist Critical Theory and Theatre*. Baltimore, MD, 1990.

Creekmur, Corey K. and Alexander Doty (ed.). *Out in Culture: Gay, Lesbian, and Queer Essays on Popular Culture*. Durham, NC, 1995.

de Lauretis, Teresa. *The Practice of Love: Lesbian Sexuality and Perverse Desire*. Bloomington, IN, 1994.

Dollimore, Jonathan. *Sexual Dissidence: Augustine to Wilde, Freud to Foucault*. Oxford, 1991.

Duberman, Martin et al. (eds). *Hidden From History: Reclaiming the Gay and Lesbian Past*. New York, 1989.

Dyer, Richard. *Gays and Film*, rev. edn. New York, 1984.

Dyer, Richard. *Now You See It: Studies on Lesbian and Gay Film*. London, 1990.

Faderman, Lillian. *Surpassing the Love of Men: Romantic Friendship and Love Between Women from the Renaissance to the Present*. New York, 1981.

Foucault, Michel. *History of Sexuality: Volume I, An Introduction*. New York, 1978.

Fuss, Diana. *Essentially Speaking: Feminism, Nature and Difference*. New York, 1989.

Fuss, Diana (ed.). *Inside/Out: Lesbian Theories, Gay Theories*. New York, 1991.

Halberstam, Judith. *Female Masculinity*. Durham, NC, 1998.

Hobby, Elaine and Chris White (eds). *What Lesbians Do in Books*. London, 1991.

Katz, Jonathan Ned. *Gay American History: Lesbians and Gay Men in the USA; A Documentary*. New York, 1976.

Martin, Robert K. *The Homosexual Tradition in American Poetry*. Austin, TX, 1979.

Mercer, Kobena. *Welcome to the Jungle: New Positions in Black Cultural Studies*. New York, 1994.

Meyers, Jeffrey. *Homosexuality and Literature*. London, 1977.

Miller, D. A. *The Novel and the Police*. Berkeley, CA, 1988.

Plummer, Kenneth (ed.). *The Making of the Modern Homosexual*. Totowa, 1981.

Plummer, Kenneth (ed.). *Modern Homosexualities: Fragments of Lesbian and Gay Experience*. London, 1992.

Porter, Kevin and Jeffrey Weeks (eds). *Between the Acts: Lives of Homosexual Men 1885 to 1967*. London, 1997.

Sandfort, Theo et al. *Lesbian and Gay Studies*. London, 2000.

Sedgwick, Eve Kosofsky. *Between Men: English Literature and Male Homosocial Desire*. New York, 1985.

Sedgwick, Eve Kosofsky. *Epistemology of the Closet*. Berkeley, CA, 1990.

Shepherd, Simon. *Because We're Queers: The Life and Crimes of Kenneth Halliwell and Joe Orton.* London, 1989.

Simpson, Mark (ed.). *Anti-Gay.* London, 1996.

Sinfield, Alan. *Cultural Politics – Queer Reading.* Philadelphia, 1994.

Sinfield, Alan. *The Wilde Century.* New York, 1994.

Sinfield, Alan. *Gay and After.* London, 1998.

Smith, Anna Marie. *New Right Discourse on Race and Sexuality: Britain 1968–1990.* Cambridge, 1994.

Smith-Rosenberg, Carroll. *Disorderly Conduct: Visions of Gender in Victorian America.* New York, 1985.

Smyth, Cherry. *Lesbians Talk Queer Notions.* London, 1992.

Still, Judith, and Michael Worten (eds). *Textuality and Sexuality: Reading Theories and Practices.* Manchester, 1993.

Van Leer, David. *The Queening of America: Gay Culture in Straight Society.* New York, 1995.

Warner, Michael (ed.). *Fear of a Queer Planet: Queer Politics and Social Theory.* Minneapolis, MN, 1993.

Weeks, Jeffrey. *Coming Out: Homosexual Politics in Britain from the Nineteenth Century to the Present.* London, 1977.

Weeks, Jeffrey. *Sex, Politics and Society: The Regulation of Sexuality Since 1800.* London, 1981.

Weeks, Jeffrey. *Sexuality and Its Discontents: Meaning, Myths and Modern Sexualities.* London, 1985.

Weeks, Jeffrey. *Against Nature: Essays on History, Sexuality and Identity.* London, 1991.

Marxism

Derived from the political, economic and philosophical texts of Karl Marx (even though Marx himself never published a specifically directed analysis of matters of aesthetics or literature), marxist literary and cultural theories and praxes are concerned primarily with the relationships between literature, culture and society. Marxist critics seek to situate texts politically and historically, whether in the written forms of novels, plays or poetry or in other forms such as film and television. Earlier models of marxist analyses saw texts as simply 'reflections' of society, basing this assumption on a possible relationship to the economic model of Base/Superstructure determined in the text of Marx. However, this 'crude' model of marxist analysis has been abandoned largely in favour of a more complex comprehension of the

political, ideological and historical mediations of the text. At its
broadest, the influence of marxism has produced in critics a
'sociological consciousness'. Matters of materiality and ideology
inform the interrogations of marxist literary criticism in its
various guises.

Bibliography

Adorno, Theodor W. et al. *Aesthetics and Politics*. London, 1980.
Althusser, Louis. *For Marx*, trans. Ben Brewster. New York, 1970.
Althusser, Louis. *Lenin and Philosophy, and Other Essays*, trans. Ben
    Brewster. London, 1971.
Althusser, Louis and Etienne Balibar. *Reading Capital*, trans. Ben
    Brewster. London, 1975.
Anderson, Perry. *Considerations on Western Marxism*. London, 1976.
Arvon, Henri. *Marxist Esthetics*, trans. Helen Lane. Ithaca, NY, 1973.
Barrett, Michèle. *The Politics of Truth: From Marx to Foucault*. Oxford,
    1991.
Benton, Ted. *The Rise and Fall of Structuralist Marxism*. London,
    1984.
Bottomore, Tom et al. (ed.). *A Dictionary of Marxist Thought*. Cam-
    bridge, MA, 1983.
Burnham, Clint. *The Jamesonian Unconscious: The Aesthetics of Marx-
    ist Theory*. Durham, NC, 1995.
Eagleton, Terry. *Criticism and Ideology: A Study in Marxist Literary
    Theory*. London, 1976.
Eagleton, Terry. *Marxism and Literary Criticism*. London, 1976.
Eagleton, Terry. *Walter Benjamin: or Towards a Revolutionary Criti-
    cism*. London, 1981.
Eagleton, Terry. *The Function of Criticism: From 'The Spectator' to
    Post-Structuralism*. London, 1984.
Frow, John. *Marxism and Literary Criticism*. Cambridge, 1986.
Goldstein, Philip. *The Politics of Literary Theory: An Introduction to
    Marxist Criticism*. Tallahassee, 1990.
Gramsci, Antonio. *Selections from Political Writings, 1910–1920*, ed.
    Quintin Hoare. London, 1977.
Gramsci, Antonio. *Selections from Political Writings, 1921–1926*, ed.
    Quintin Hoare. London, 1978.
Gramsci, Antonio. *Selections from the Cultural Writings*, eds. David
    Forgacs and Geoffrey Nowell Smith. London, 1985.
Gramsci, Antonio. *Prison Notebooks. Vols 1 and 2*, trans. and ed. Joseph
    Buttigieg. New York, 1992.

MARXISM 135

Haslett, Moyra. Marxist Literary and Cultural Theories. Basingstoke, 2000.
Homer, Sean. *Fredric Jameson: Marxism, Hermeneutics, Postmodernism.* New York, NY, 1998.
Jameson, Fredric. *Marxism and Form.* New Jersey, 1971.
Jameson, Fredric. *The Political Unconscious.* Ithaca, NY, 1981.
Jay, Martin. *Marxism and Totality: The Adventures of a Concept from Lukács to Habermas.* Berkeley, CA, 1984.
Johnson, Pauline. *Marxist Aesthetics.* London, 1984.
Lukàcs, György. *The Historical Novel.* New York, 1962.
Lukács, György. *History and Class Consciousness,* trans. Rodney Livingstone. Cambridge, 1971.
Macherey, Pierre. *A Theory of Literary Production,* trans. Geoffrey Wall. London, 1978.
Macherey, Pierre. *In a Materialist Way: Selected Essays,* ed. Warren Montag, trans. Ted Stolze. London, 1998.
Marx, Karl. *Selected Writings,* ed. David McLellan. Oxford, 1977.
Marx, Karl. *Capital* Vols 1–3, trans. Ben Fowkes (vol. 1), David Fernbach (vols 2 and 3), intro. Ernest Mandel. London, 1990–92.
Marx, Karl *Grundrisse,* trans. Martin Nicolaus. London, 1993.
Marx, Karl (with Friedrich Engels). *The German Ideology: Students' Edition,* ed. and intro. C. J. Arthur. London, 1970.
Marx, Karl (with Friedrich Engels). *The Communist Manifesto,* intro. A. J. P. Taylor. London, 1985.
Mulhern, Francis. *Contemporary Marxist Literary Criticism.* Harlow, 1992.
Nelson, Cary and Grossberg, Lawrence (eds). *Marxism and the Interpretation of Culture.* Urbana, IL, 1988.
Solomon, Maynard (ed.). *Marxism and Art: Essays Classic and Contemporary.* New York, 1973.
Williams, Raymond. *Culture and Society 1780–1950.* London, 1958.
Williams, Raymond. *The Long Revolution.* London, 1961.
Williams, Raymond. *Communications.* Harmondsworth, 1962.
Williams, Raymond. *Television: Technology and Cultural Form.* New York, 1975.
Williams, Raymond. *Marxism and Literature.* Oxford, 1977.
Williams, Raymond. *Problems in Materialism and Culture: Selected Essays.* London, 1980.
Williams, Raymond. *Towards 2000.* London, 1983.
Williams, Raymond. *Resources of Hope.* London, 1989.
Wood, Ellen Meiksins. *The Retreat from Class: A New 'True' Socialism.* London, 1986.
Wood, Ellen Meiksins and John Bellamy Foster (eds). *Defense of History: Marxism and the Postmodern Agenda.* New York, 1997.

New Criticism

The new criticism came to be defined principally by the work of John Crowe Ransom, Allen Tate, R. P. Blackmur, Robert Penn Warren and Cleanth Brooks, whose reading of literature shared a focus on form and on the individual experience of the text, rather than on matters of historical and cultural context or mediation. Implicitly rejecting historical and philological scholarship which was prominent in the 1930s in North American universities' study of literature, the new criticism, exercised enormous influence on the study of literature until at least the late 1960s, and, indeed, beyond that. The new criticism, emphasising the reading of individual texts within an implicit framework of humanist belief, analyses texts with a view to showing the organic unity of a text, based on the careful explication through close reading of predominant thematic and figural textual elements.

Bibliography

Bové, Paul. *Intellectuals in Power: A Genealogy of Critical Humanism.* New York, 1986.

Brooks, Cleanth. *An Approach to Literature*, rev. edn. New York, 1939.

Brooks, Cleanth. *Modern Poetry and the Tradition.* Chapel Hill, NC, 1939.

Brooks, Cleanth. *The Well-Wrought Urn: Studies in the Structure of Poetry.* New York, 1947.

Brooks, Cleanth. *The Hidden God: Studies in Hemingway, Faulkner, Yeats, Eliot, and Warren.* New Haven, CT, 1963.

Brooks, Cleanth and Robert Penn Warren. *Modern Rhetoric.* New York, 1949.

Fekete, John. *The Critical Twilight: Explorations in the Ideology of Anglo-American Literary Theory from Eliot to McLuhan.* London, 1978.

Graff, Gerald. *Professing Literature: An Institutional History.* Chicago, 1987.

Jancovich, Mark. *The Cultural Politics of the New Criticism.* Cambridge, 1993.

Janssen, Marian. *The Kenyon Review 1939–1970: A Critical History.* Baton Rouge, LA, 1990.

Krieger, Murray. *The New Apologists for Poetry*. Minneapolis, MN, 1956.

Lentricchia, Frank. *After the New Criticism*. London, 1983.

Ransom, John Crowe. *God Without Thunder: An Unorthodox Defense of Orthodoxy*. 1931.

Ransom, John Crowe. *The World's Body*. New York, 1938.

Spurlin, William J. and Michael Fischer (eds). *The New Criticism and Contemporary Literary Theory*. New York, 1995.

Tate, Allen (ed.). *The Language of Poetry*. New Haven, 1963.

Twelve Southerners. *I'll Take my Stand: The South and the Agrarian Tradition*. Baton Rouge, LA, 1980.

Warren, Robert Penn. *Selected Essays*. New York, 1958.

Wimsatt, W. K. and Cleanth Brooks. *Literary Criticism: a Short History*. New York, 1957.

Winchell, Mark Royden. *Cleanth Brooks and the Rise of Modern Criticism*. Charlottesville, VA, 1996.

New Historicism

Prominent in the 1980s, the new historicism emerged in North America as a critical methodology which politicised and stressed the intimate interrelationship between literature, culture and history. Focusing on a wide range of tropes and concepts, including figures of the body, incarceration and subjection, amongst others, new historicists read textual formations as the complex mediation of ideological, epistemological and discursive investments. While rejecting overarching models of analysis, new historicism addressed the question of text and history not as a relationship of text and context or foreground and background, but instead insisted on an understanding of the text as a privileged moment within a network of discursive and material praxes. Furthermore, the new historicism seeks to de-emphasise the conventional privileging of the literary over non-literary text; thus letters, legal and political documents, journals and so on all belong to the network of cultural inscription at any given historical moment. While interests among new historicists are wide-ranging, what is arguably typical of the new historicist analysis is the focus in the reading of the text on the ways in which a text produces a subversive critique of dominant ideologies from the period in which it is produced, only to find that subversion ultimately recuperated and contained by the conservative powers against which it has sought to act and articulate itself.

Bibliography

Brannigan, John. *New Historicism and Cultural Materialism*. Basingstoke, 1998.

Colebrook, Claire. *New Literary Histories: New Historicism and Contemporary Criticism*. Manchester, 1997.

Foucault, Michel. *The Order of Things: An Archaeology of the Human Sciences*. New York, 1970.

Gallagher, Catherine. *The Industrial Reformation of English Fiction: Social Discourse and Narrative Form 1832–1867*. Chicago, 1985.

Gallagher, Catherine and Stephen Greenblatt. *Practicing the New Historicism*. Chicago, 2000.

Goldberg, Jonathan. *James I and the Politics of Literature: Johnson, Shakespeare, Donne and their Contemporaries*. Baltimore, MD, 1983.

Greenblatt, Stephen J. *Sir Walter Ralegh: The Renaissance Man and His Roles*. New Haven, CT, 1973.

Greenblatt, Stephen. *Renaissance Self-Fashioning from More to Shakespeare*. Chicago, 1980.

Greenblatt, Stephen J. *Shakespearean Negotiations: The Circulation of Social Energy in Renaissance England*. Berkeley, CA, 1988.

Greenblatt, Stephen J. *Learning to Curse: Essays in Early Modern Culture*. New York, 1990.

Greenblatt, Stephen J. *Marvellous Possessions: The Wonder of the New World*. Chicago, 1991.

Howard, Jean E. *The Stage and Social Struggle in Early Modern England*. London, 1994.

Montrose, Louis Adrian. 'Renaissance Literary Studies and the Subject of History', *English Literary Renaissance*, 16 (1986).

Montrose, Louis Adrian. *The Purpose of Playing: Shakespeare and the Cultural Politics of The Elizabethan Theatre*. Chicago, 1996.

Orgel, Stephen. *The Illusion of Power: Political Theatre in the Renaissance*. Berkeley, CA, 1975.

Veeser, H. Aram (ed.). *The New Historicism Reader*. London, 1984.

Veeser, H. Aram (ed.). *The New Historicism*. New York, 1989.

Wilson, Richard and Richard Dutton (eds). *New Historicism and Renaissance Drama*. Harlow, 1992.

Phenomenology

Developed from the branch of philosophy inaugurated by Edmund Husserl, phenomenological criticism treats works of art, such as the novel, as those works exist and have and are given meaning in the consciousness, perception and awareness of their readers or audience prior to any supposed objective reality. Phenomenology proposes a comprehension of the world which does not separate the subjective experience of the world from the objects experienced. Phenomenological criticism thus stresses the affective aspects of the text, and the ways in which the reader's imagination develops awareness of, and thus communicates with, the text in question. There is both a linguistic and psychological aspect to phenomenology which makes it available for literary criticism in particular ways, given that the reader's imagination, and the language through which that interpretation is shaped, govern perception *as* interpretation. The text no longer has an independent or universal meaning, and, moreover, meaning cannot be controlled by the author.

Bibliography

Bernasconi, Robert. *The Question of Language in Heidegger's History of Being*. New Jersey, 1985.

Bernet, Rudolf et al. *An Introduction to Husserlian Phänomenologie*. Evanston, IL, 1993.

Derrida, Jacques. *Speech and Phenomena and Other Essays on Husserl's Theory of Signs*, trans. and intro. David B. Allison. Preface Newton Garver. Evanston, IL, 1973.

Derrida, Jacques. *Edmund Husserl's Origin of Geometry: An Introduction*, trans., preface, and afterword, John P. Leavey, Jr. Lincoln, NE, 1989.

Gadamer, Hans-Georg. *Truth and Method*, 2nd rev. edn. trans. Joel Weinsheimer and Donald G. Marshall. New York, 1989.

Hegel, G. W. F. *Phenomenology of Spirit*, trans. A. V. Miller. Oxford, 1977.

Heidegger, Martin. *Being and Time*, trans. John Macquarrie and Edward Robinson. Oxford, 1962.

Heidegger, Martin. *Poetry, Language, Thought*, trans. and intro. Albert Hofstadter. New York, 1971.

Heidegger, Martin. *On the Way to Language*, trans. Peter D. Hertz. New York, 1982.

Heidegger, Martin. *History of the Concept of Time: Prolegomena*, trans. Theodore Kisiel. Bloomington, IN, 1985.

Husserl, Edmund. *Cartesian Meditations: An Introduction to Phenomenology*, trans. Dorian Cairns. The Hague, 1960.

Husserl, Edmund. *The Crisis of European Sciences and Transcendental Phenomenology: An Introduction to Phenomenological Philosophy*, trans. David Carr. Evanston, IL, 1970.

Husserl, Edmund. *The Idea of Phenomenology*, trans. William P. Alston and George Nakhnikian, intro. George Nakhnikian. The Hague, 1973.

Husserl, Edmund. *Ideas Pertaining to a Pure Phenomenology and to a Phenomenological Philosophy*, Vol 1, trans. F. Kersten. The Hague, 1982.

Ingarden, Roman. *The Cognition of the Literary Work of Art: An Investigation on the Borderlines of Ontology, Logic, and Theory of Literature*, trans. Ruth Ann Crowley and Kenneth R. Olson. Evanston, IL, 1973.

Jauss, Hans Robert. *Aesthetic Experience and Literary Hermeneutics*, trans. Michael Shaw, intro. Wlad Godzich. Minneapolis, MN, 1982.

Lyotard, Jean-François. *Phenomenology*, trans. Brian Beakley, foreword Gayle L. Ormiston. Albany, NY, 1991.

Merleau-Ponty, Maurice. *The Primacy of Perception and other Essays on Phenomenological Psychology, the Philosophy of Art, History, and Politics*, trans., ed. and intro. James M. Edie. Evanston, IL, 1964

Ricœur, Paul. *The Conflict of Interpretations Essays in Hermeneutics*, trans. and ed. Don Ihde. Evanston, IL, 1974.

Ricœur, Paul. *The Rule of Metaphor: Multi-Disciplinary Studies of the Creation of Meaning in Language*, trans. Robert Czerny, with Kathleen McLaughlin and John Costello. Toronto, 1977.

Sallis, John. *Delimitations: Phenomenology and the End of Metaphysics*. Bloomington, IN, 1986.

Sartre, Jean-Paul. *What is Literature*, trans. Bernard Frechtman. New York, 1966.

Sartre, Jean-Paul. *Being and Nothingness*, trans. Hazel E. Barnes, intro. Mary Warnock. London, 1969.

Postmarxism

Largely identified as a movement with the work of Ernesto Laclau and Chantal Mouffe (and to a certain extent with the psychoanalytically inflected political critique of Slavoj Žižek), postmarxism names a radical effort to move beyond orthodox models of marxist critique through an engagement with the philosophical and textual interests of particular strands of critical thinking identified as poststructuralist or deconstructive, so called. Drawing from the work of Derrida and Lacan, amongst others, Laclau and Mouffe have privileged notions of difference and contingency in challenging determinist models of economic thought. They also provided provocative and often cogent critiques of tendencies within marxism towards universalism, reductionism and functionalism in the name of a pluralist marxism, although the radical relativism of Laclau and Mouffe's earlier publications (from which position they have partly retreated in the face of criticism) has been seen as problematic for the purposes of political praxis.

Bibliography

Laclau, Ernesto. *Politics and Ideology in Marxist Theory.* London, 1977.

Laclau, Ernesto. *New Reflections on the Revolution of Our Time.* London, 1990.

Laclau, Ernesto (ed.). *The Making of Political Identities.* London, 1994.

Laclau, Ernesto. *Emancipation(s).* London, 1996.

Laclau, Ernesto and Chantal Mouffe. *Hegemony and Socialist Strategy: Towards a Radical Democratic Politics.* London, 1985.

Laclau, Ernesto, Chantal Mouffe, Judith Butler and Slavoj Žižek. *Contingency, Hegemony, Universality: Contemporary Dialogues on the Left.* London, 2000.

Mouffe, Chantal (ed.). *Dimensions of Radical Democracy: Pluralism, Citizenship, Community.* London, 1992.

Mouffe, Chantal. *The Return of The Political.* London, 1993.

Mouffe, Chantal. *The Challenge of Carl Schmitt.* London, 1999.

Mouffe, Chantal. *The Democratic Paradox.* London, 2000.

Sim, Stuart (ed.). *Post-Marxism: A Reader.* Edinburgh, 1998.

Smith, Anna Marie. *Laclau and Mouffe: The Radical Democratic Imaginary.* London, 1998.

Torfing, J. *New Theories of Discourse: Laclau, Mouffe and Žižek.* London, 1999.

Postmodernism

While there is little consensus over the meaning of postmodernism, it may be suggested, albeit provisionally, that postmodernist literary criticism is concerned not only with the status of the literary artefact, but also with matters of language, representation, identity, origin and truth. More sweepingly, postmodernism has been defined by Jean-François Lyotard as an attitude of suspicion towards the grand narratives of history. If history has always been written by the victors, postmodernist scepticism points to the fact that history is a narrativisation and not a truth, and that, furthermore, there are competing narratives, none of which may claim any greater veracity than any of their competitors. Although becoming an established, if contested, term for experimental writing by the early 1970s, earliest uses in English date back to the late 1940s as a definition for a style of architecture and, subsequently, with regard to writings which exhibited aesthetics best described as anti-modernist and anti-rationalist. Part of the purpose of postmodern practice was to destabilise distinctions between high and popular culture, which much modernism in the arts had sought to emphasise and maintain. Subsequently in the late 1970s and 1980s postmodernism became confused with the equally vague term *poststructuralism*, particularly the alleged emphasis on the part of the latter phenomenon with textuality and play. Lyotard's *The Postmodern Condition* has been a key philosophical text serving to emphasise the politics of postmodernity beyond the oversimplified assumptions concerning play and destabilisation within a purely semantic or linguistic realm. For Lyotard and, subsequently, cultural and literary critics such as Jean Baudrillard and Fredric Jameson, postmodernism named the hegemonic cultural logic of technologically advanced Western societies. In this understanding was incorporated critical response to the phenomena of post-industrial consumerism, multinational capitalism, and the role of simulacra and simulations which alienate the subject from any possible direct relationship to reality. It has been this turn to the political which has revitalised postmodern critical analysis in the last decade.

Bibliography

Amiram, Eyal and John Unsworth (eds). *Essays in Postmodern Culture.* New York, 1993.

Appignanesi, Lisa (ed.). *Postmodernism: ICA Documents.* London, 1989.

Baudrillard, Jean. *Simulations.* Trans. Paul Foss et al. New York, 1983.

Baudrillard, Jean. *Jean Baudrillard: Selected Writings,* ed. Mark Poster. Stanford, CA, 1988.

Bauman, Zygmunt. *Postmodern Ethics.* Oxford, 1993.

Benhabib Seyla. *Situating the Self: Gender, Community and Postmodernism in Contemporary Ethics.* Cambridge, 1992.

Bertens, Hans. *The Idea of the Postmodern: A History.* London, 1995.

Bertens, Hans and Douwe Fokkema (eds). *International Post-modernism: Theory and Literary Practice.* Amsterdam, 1996.

Best, Steven, and Douglas Kellner. *Postmodern Theory: Critical Interrogations.* New York, 1991.

Bewes, Timothy. *Cynicism and Postmodernity.* London, 1997.

Calinescu, Matei. *Five Faces of Modernity: Modernism, Avant-Garde, Decadence, Kitsch, Postmodernism.* Durham, NC, 1987.

Callinicos, Alex. *Against Postmodernism: A Marxist Critique.* New York, 1989.

Connor, Steven. *Postmodern Culture: An Introduction to the Theories of the Contemporary.* Oxford, 1989.

Currie, Mark. *Postmodern Narrative Theory.* Basingstoke, 1998.

Dellamora, Richard (ed.). *Postmodern Apocalypse: Theory and Cultural Practice at the End.* Philadelphia, 1996.

D'haen, Theo and Hans Bertens (eds). *'Closing the Gap': American Postmodern Fiction in Germany, Italy, Spain, and the Netherlands.* Amsterdam, 1997.

Durham, Scott. *Phantom Communities: The Simulacrum and the Limits of Postmodernism.* Stanford, CA, 1998.

Ebert, Teresa L. *Ludic Feminism and After: Postmodernism, Desire, and Labor in Late Capitalism.* Ann Arbor, MI, 1996.

Elam, Diane. *Romancing the Postmodern.* New York, 1992.

Federman, Raymond. *Critifiction: Postmodern Essays.* Albany, NY, 1993.

Foster, Hal (ed.). *The Anti-Aesthetic: Essays in Postmodern Culture.* Port Townsend, 1983.

Foster, Hal. (ed.). *Postmodern Culture.* London, 1985.

Harvey, David. *The Condition of Postmodernity.* London, 1993.

Hogue, Lawrence W. *Race, Modernity, Postmodernity: A Look at the*

History and Literatures of People of Color Since the 1960s. Albany, NY, 1996.

Hutcheon, Linda. *A Poetics of Postmodernism: History, Theory, Fiction.* New York, 1988.

Hutcheon, Linda. *The Politics of Postmodernism.* New York, 1989.

Jameson, Fredric. *Postmodernism, or, the Cultural Logic of Late Capitalism.* Durham, NL, 1991.

Klinkowitz, Jerry. *Literary Disruptions: The Making of Post-Contemporary American Fiction,* 2nd edn. Urbana, IL, 1980.

Leitch, Vincent B. *Postmodernism: Local Effects, Global Flows.* Albany, NY, 1996.

Lucy, Niall. *Postmodern Literary Theory: An Introduction.* Oxford, 1997.

Lyotard, Jean-François. *The Postmodern Condition: A Report on Knowledge,* trans. Geoff Bennington and Brian Massumi. Minneapolis, MN, 1984.

Lyotard, Jean-François. *The Postmodern Explained,* trans. Don Barry et al., eds. Julian Pefanis and Morgan Thomas, afterword Wlad Godzich. Minneapolis, MN, 1992.

Marshall, Brenda K. *Teaching the Postmodern: Fiction and Theory.* New York, 1992.

McHale, Brian. *Postmodern Fiction.* New York, 1987.

McHale, Brian. *Constructing Postmodernism.* New York, 1992.

Maltby, Paul. *Dissident Postmodernists: Barthelme, Coover, Pynchon.* Philadelphia, 1991.

Newman, Charles. *The Post-Modern Aura: The Act of Fiction in an Age of Inflation.* Evanston, IL, 1985.

Nicholson, Linda J. (ed.). *Feminism/Postmodernism.* New York, 1990.

Sarup, Madan. *Identity, Culture, and the Postmodern World.* Athens, OH, 1996.

Soja, Edward. *Postmodern Geographies.* London, 1989.

Poststructuralism

Not a movement per se, but rather, initially, an Anglo-American perception of common strands in continental thought, particularly in the fields of psychoanalysis, feminism, marxism, philosophy, linguistics, and literary and cultural criticism, poststructuralism names loosely the reception and deployment of these various diverse and heterogeneous strands (from the work, for example, of Althusser, Barthes, Cixous, Derrida, Irigaray, Kristeva, Lacan) as they have come to be translated and transformed through the Anglo-American theorising of questions of the literary and the matter of critical, textual analysis. The terms *poststructuralism* and *theory* or *high theory* have been assumed by some to be virtually synonymous (as have *poststructuralism* and *deconstruction*), and the salient discernible features in common of this so-called critical modality – allegedly – have to do with the following topics: the work of rhetoric, the destabilising effects of language, the provisionality of meaning, the work of tropes and images in resisting uniformity or organic wholeness, questions of undecidability, discontinuity, the aporetic and fragmentation, difference and otherness, the constructedness of the subject, matters of translation, and the denial or, perhaps more accurately, a critique of the referentiality or mimetic function of language.

Bibliography

Attridge, Derek. *Peculiar Language: Literature as Difference from the Renaissance to James Joyce*. Ithaca, NY, 1988.

Attridge, Derek and Daniel Ferrer (eds). *Post-Structuralist Joyce: Essays from the French*. Cambridge, 1984.

Attridge, Derek, Geoffrey Bennington and Robert Young (eds). *Post-Structuralism and the Question of History*. Cambridge, 1987.

Chase, Cynthia. *Decomposing Figures: Rhetorical Readings in the Romantic Tradition*. Baltimore, MD, 1986.

Cohen, Tom. *Anti-Mimesis from Plato to Hitchcock*. Cambridge, 1995.

Cohen, Tom. *Ideology and Inscription: 'Cultural Studies' After Benjamin, De Man, and Bakhtin*. Cambridge, 1998.

De Man, Paul. *Allegories of Reading: Figural Language in Rousseau, Nietzsche, Rilke, and Proust*. New Haven, CT, 1979.

De Man, Paul. *The Rhetoric of Romanticism*. New York, 1984.

De Man, Paul. *The Resistance to Theory*. Minneapolis, MN, 1986.

de Man, Paul. *Aesthetic Ideology*, ed. and intro. Andrzej Warminski. Minneapolis, 1996.

Easthope, Antony. *Poetry as Discourse*. London, 1983.

Easthope, Antony. *British Poststructuralism since 1968*. London, 1988.

Harari, Josué V. (ed.). *Textual Strategies: Perspectives in Post-Structuralist Criticism*. London, 1979.

Johnson, Barbara. *The Critical Difference*. Baltimore, MD, 1980.

MacCabe, Colin. *James Joyce and the Revolution of the Word*. London, 1978.

Niranjana, Tejaswini. *Siting Translation: History, Post-Structuralism, and the Colonial Context*. Berkeley, CA, 1992.

Ronell, Avital. *The Telephone Book: Technology, Schizophrenia, Electric Speech*. Lincoln, NE, 1989.

Ronell, Avital. *Crack Wars: Literature, Addiction, Mania*. Lincoln, NE, 1992.

Pepper, Thomas. *Singularities: Extremes of Theory in the Twentieth Century*. Cambridge, 1997.

Weedon, Chris. *Feminist Practice and Poststructuralist Theory*. Oxford, 1987.

Young, Robert (ed.). *Untying the Text: A Post-Structuralist Reader*. London, 1981.

Psychoanalytic Criticism

Psychoanalytic criticism is derived, largely, from the work, first, of Sigmund Freud, and, subsequently, Jacques Lacan, although not exclusively. Particularly with regard to the complexities of the Lacanian text, and its often contentious analysis of female sexuality, there has emerged a sustained, critical interest in the stakes of psychoanalysis for feminism, particularly in relation to the location and constitution of the female subject within and by patriarchal cultural and psychic structures. The work of Hélène Cixous, Luce Irigaray and Julia Kristeva has provided much of the impetus for feminist re-evaluation. While there is no *one* psychoanalytic literary criticism, no single analytical mode, where the interests of analysis intersect is in the interest of the constitution of the psychic structures of the text; the text is read as giving access to psychic structures, not by what is expressed but by that which is avoided, which is passed over in silence, which is articulated ambivalently, and which is focused rhetorically in particularly intense fashion. Moreover, for psychoanalytic criticism in its analysis of the textual subject (and the subject or identity as textual, as constructed through layers of language), the interest is how the text operates beneath and, often, *despite* what it appears to say. Themes and motifs central to psychoanalytic criticism are desire and loss, delay and repetition or doubling, forms of prohibition, lack, sexual sublimation or repression, and the sexual drive hidden within acts and events which are not obviously sexual in nature.

Bibliography

Adams, Parveen. *The Emptiness of the Image: Psychoanalysis and Sexual Differences.* London, 1996.

Adams, Parveen and Elizabeth Cowie (eds). *The Woman in Question: m/f.* Cambridge, MA, 1990.

Apollon, Willy and Richard Feldstein (eds). *Lacan, Politics, Aesthetics.* Albany, NY, 1996.

Bloom, Harold. *The Anxiety of Influence: A Theory of Poetry.* New York, 1973.

Bloom, Harold. *Agon: Towards a Theory of Revisionism.* New York, 1982.

Brennan, Teresa (ed.). *Between Feminism and Psychoanalysis.* London, 1989.

Brooks, Peter. *Reading for the Plot: Design and Intention in Narrative.* New York, 1984.

Brooks, Peter. *Psychoanalysis and Storytelling.* London, 1994.

Bowie, Malcolm. *Freud, Proust and Lacan.* 1987.

Bowie, Malcolm. *Lacan.* London, 1991.

Bowie, Malcolm. *Psychoanalysis and the Future of Theory.* Oxford, 1991.

Davis, Robert Con (ed.). *The Fictional Father: Lacanian Readings of the Text.* Amherst, 1981.

Davis, Robert Con (ed.). *Lacan and Narration: The Psychoanalytic Difference in Narrative Theory.* Baltimore, MD, 1983.

Donald, James (ed.). *Psychoanalysis and Cultural Theory: Thresholds.* London, 1991.

Easthope, Antony. *Literary into Cultural Studies.* London, 1991.

Easthope, Antony. *The Unconscious.* London, 1999.

Elliott, Anthony and Stephen Frosh (eds). *Psychoanalysis in Contexts: Paths Between Theory and Modern Culture.* London, 1995.

Ellmann, Maud (ed.). *Psychoanalytic Literary Criticism.* London, 1994.

Feldstein, Richard and Judith Roof (eds). *Feminism and Psychoanalysis.* Ithaca, NY, 1989.

Felman, Shoshana (ed.). *Literature and Psychoanalysis: The Question of Reading: Otherwise.* Baltimore, MD, 1982.

Fletcher, John and Andrew Benjamin (eds). *Abjection, Melancholia, and Love: The Work of Julia Kristeva.* London, 1990.

Freud, Sigmund. *The Standard Edition of the Complete Psychoanalytic Works of Sigmund Freud*. 24 vols, ed. and trans. James Strachey. London, 1953–74.

Gallop, Jane. *The Daughter's Seduction: Feminism and Psychoanalysis*. Ithaca, NY, 1982.

Grosz, Elizabeth. *Jacques Lacan: A Feminist Introduction*. London, 1990.

Hartman, Geoffrey (ed.). *Psychoanalysis and the Question of the Text*. Baltimore, MD, 1978.

Hertz, Neil. *The End of the Line: Essays on Psychoanalysis and the Sublime*. New York, 1985.

Holland, Norman N. *Holland's Guide to Psychoanalytic Psychology and Literature-and-Psychology*. New York, 1990.

Jacobus, Mary. *Reading Women*. London, 1987.

Johnson, Barbara. *The Feminist Difference: Literature, Psychoanalysis, Race, and Gender*. Cambridge, 1998.

Kaplan, E. Ann. *Psychoanalysis and Cinema*. London, 1990.

Lacan, Jacques. *Ecrits: A Selection*, trans. Alan Sheridan, ed. Jacques-Alain Miller, intro. David Macey. London, 1977.

Lacan, Jacques. *The Four Fundamental Concepts of Psycho-analysis*, trans. Alan Sheridan. Ed. Jacques-Alain Miller, intro. David Macey. London, 1994.

Lechte, John (ed.). *Writing and Psychoanalysis: A Reader*. London, 1996.

Lupton, Julia Reinhard and Kenneth Reinhard. *After Oedipus: Shakespeare in Psychoanalysis*. Ithaca, NY, 1993.

MacCannell, Juliet Flower. *Figuring Lacan: Criticism and the Cultural Unconscious*. London, 1986.

Massardier-Kenney, Françoise (ed.). *Lacanian Theory of Discourse: Subject, Structure, Society*. London, 1994.

Mitchell, Juliet. *Psychoanalysis and Feminism*. London, 1974.

Mitchell, Juliet and Rose, Jacqueline (eds). *Feminine Sexuality: Jacques Lacan and the école freudienne*. London, 1982.

Muller, John P. and William J. Richardson. *The Purloined Poe: Lacan, Derrida, and Psychoanalytic Reading*. Baltimore, MD, 1988.

Mulvey, Laura. *Visual and Other Pleasures*. London, 1989.

Ragland-Sullivan, Ellie and Mark Bracher (eds). *Lacan and the Subject of Language*. London, 1991.

Rose, Jacqueline. *Sexuality in the Field of Vision*. London, 1986.

Rose, Jacqueline. *The Haunting of Sylvia Plath*. London, 1991.

Rose, Jacqueline. *Why War? Psychoanalysis, Politics and the Return to Melanie Klein*. Oxford, 1993.

Schwartz, Murray M. and Coppelia Kahn (eds). *Representing Shakespeare: New Psychoanalytic Essays*. Baltimore, MD, 1980.

Sedgwick, Eve. *Between Men: English Literature and Male Homosocial Desire*. New York, 1985.

Shamdasani, Sonu and Michael Münchow (eds). *Speculations After Freud: Psychoanalysis, Philosophy and Culture*. London, 1994.

Skura, Meredith Anne. *The Literary Use of the Psychoanalytic Process*. New Haven, CT, 1981.

Weber, Samuel. *The Legend of Freud*. Minneapolis, MN, 1982.

Wright, Elizabeth. *Psychoanalytic Criticism: Theory in Practice*, 2nd edn. Cambridge, 1998.

Žižek, Slavoj. *The Sublime Object of Ideology*. London, 1989.

Reader-Response Theory/Reception Theory

Reader-Response and Reception Theory theorise that the responses of readers over a given period of time determine the various ways in which they find meaning and value through literary texts. Reader-response critics contend that literary works do not function as self-contained, autonomous objects, but rather as realities that become established by the readers who consume them. Theorists often conceive of this process as the product of phenomenology, or the emergence, via our shared consciousness, of the textual objects that we perceive. Theorists such as Stanley Fish, for example, conceive of the notion of a reader-response criticism in terms of a given text's psychological effects, while other thinkers such as Norman Holland and David Bleich define the movement's aim in terms of the text's self-reflexive and ultimately subjective possibilities.

Reception theory – or *rezeptionaesthetik* – refers to the school of criticism that explores the many and often divergent ways in which literary works are received following their initial publication. Jauss utilised the concept of 'aesthetic distance' to explain the differences between a given work's immediate reception and its contemporary profile. Jauss argues, moreover, that this notion intersects with a given reader's 'horizon of expectations', or the textual elements that impact the reader's expectations regarding the text in question. There are two principal schools of thought devoted to the manner in which reception theory can be applied by literary critics. The 'Constance' school – which includes such luminaries as Jauss and Wolfgang Iser – maintains that the effect on the reader, who draws upon his or her individual experiences during the act of reading, should function as the literary critic's primary concern. The 'Geneva' school – which includes such voices as Hans Georg Gadamer and Roman Ingarden – contends that a series of 'essential conditions', or a given reader's expectations about the present and the future, inevitably impinge upon our reading experiences.

Bibliography

Bennett, Andrew (ed.). *Readers and Reading*. London, 1995.

Bleich, David. *Readings and Feelings: An Introduction to Subjective Criticism*. Urbana, IL, 1975.

Bleich, David. *Literature and Self-Awareness: Critical Questions and Emotional Responses*. New York, 1977.

Bleich, David. *Subjective Criticism*. Baltimore, MD, 1978

Eco, Umberto. *The Role of the Reader: Explorations in the Semiotics of Texts*. Bloomington, IN, 1979.

Falk, Eugene H. *The Poetics of Roman Ingarden*. Chapel Hill, NC, 1981.

Fish, Stanley. *Surprised by Sin: the Reader in 'Paradise Lost'*. London, 1967.

Fish, Stanley. *Self-Consuming Artifacts: the Experience of Seventeenth-Century Literature*. Berkeley, CA, 1972.

Fish, Stanley. *Is There A Text in This Class? The Authority of Interpretive Communities*. Cambridge, MA, 1980.

Freund, Elizabeth. *The Return of the Reader: Reader-Response Criticism*. London, 1987.

Gadamer, Hans-Georg. *The Relevance of the Beautiful and Other Essays*, trans. Nicholas Walker, ed. Robert Bernasconi. Cambridge, 1986.

Gadamer, Hans-Georg. *Truth and Method*, trans. rev. Joel Weinsheimer and Donald G. Marshall, 2nd edn. London, 1989.

Gadamer, Hans-Georg. *Gadamer on Celan: 'Who am I and Who are You?' and Other Essays*, trans. and eds Richard Heinemann and Bruce Krajewski. New York, 1997.

Garvin, Harry R. (ed.). *Theories of Reading, Looking, Listening*. Lewisburg, 1981.

Holland, Norman N. *The Dynamics of Literary Response*. New York, 1968.

Holland, Norman N. *Poems in Persons: An Introduction to the Psychoanalysis of Literature*. New York, 1973.

Holland, Norman N. *5 Readers Reading*. New Haven, CT, 1975.

Holub, Robert C. *Reception Theory: A Critical Introduction*. London, 1984.

Ingarden, Roman. *The Cognition of the Literary Work of Art*, trans. Ruth Ann Crowley and Kenneth Olson. Evanston, IL, 1973.

Ingarden, Roman. *The Literary Work of Art: An Investigation on the Borderlines of Ontology, Logic, and the Theory of Literature*, trans. and intro. George G. Grabowicz. Evanston, IL, 1973.

Ingarden, Roman. *The Ontology of the Work of Art: The Musical Work, the Picture, the Architectural Work, the Film*, trans. Raymond Meyer and John T. Goldthwait. Athens, OH, 1989.

Iser, Wolfgang. *The Implied Reader: Patterns of Communication in Prose Fiction from Bunyan to Beckett*. Baltimore, MD, 1974.

Iser, Wolfgang. *The Act of Reading: A Theory of Aesthetic Response*. London, 1978.

Iser, Wolfgang. *Prospecting: from Reader Response to Literary Anthropology*. Baltimore, MD, 1989.

Jauss, Hans Robert. *Aesthetic Experience and Literary Hermeneutics*, trans. Michael Shaw. Minneapolis, MN, 1982.

Jauss, Hans Robert. *Toward an Aesthetic of Reception*, trans. Timothy Bahti. Minneapolis, MN, 1982.

Poulet, Georges. *Studies in Human Time*, trans. Elliott Coleman. Baltimore, MD, 1956.

Purves, Alan C. and Richard Beach. *Literature and the Reader: Research in Response to Literature, Reading Interests, and the Teaching of Literature*. Urbana, IL, 1972.

Scholes, Robert. *Protocols of Reading*. New Haven, CT, 1989.

Slatoff, Walter. *With Respect to Readers: Dimensions of Literary Response*. Ithaca, NY, 1970.

Suleiman, Susan R. and Inge Crosman (eds). *The Reader in the Text: Essays on Audience and Interpretation*. Princeton, NJ, 1980.

Tompkins, Jane P. (ed.). *Reader-Response Criticism: from Formalism to Post-Structuralism*. Baltimore, MD, 1980.

Russian Formalism

Russian formalism is often associated with such figures as Victor Shklovsky, Boris Eichenbaum, Jan Mukarovsky, Yuri Tynyanov and Roman Jakobson, among others. Russian formalism resulted from the work of two groups of Russian literary critics and linguists, including the Moscow Linguistics Circle (founded in 1915) and the Society for the Study of Poetic Language (founded in St Petersburg in 1916). Russian formalists eschewed the notion that literature could best be understood in terms of such extra-literary matters as philosophy, history, sociology, biography and autobiography. Initially, they employed formalism as a derogatory term for the analysis of literature's formal structures and technical patterns. As Russian formalism's ideology became more refined, however, the concept began to assume more neutral connotations. Russian formalists – as with the Prague structuralists who would champion Russian formalism's critique after their suppression by the Soviet government in the 1930s – argue that literature functions upon a series of unique features of language that allows it to afford the reader with a mode of experience unavailable via the auspices of ordinary language.

Bibliography

Bann, Stephen and John E. Bowlt (eds). *Russian Formalism: A Collection of Articles and Texts in Translation*. New York, 1973.

Erlich, Victor. *Russian Formalism*. The Hague, 1955.

Jakobson, Roman and Morris Halle. *Fundamentals of Language*. The Hague, 1956.

Jameson, Fredric. *The Prison-House of Language: A Critical Account of Structuralism and Russian Formalism*. Princeton, NJ, 1972.

Lemon, L. T. and M. J. Reis (eds). *Russian Formalist Criticism: Four Essays*. Lincoln, NE, 1965.

Matejka, Ladislav and Krystyna Pomorska (eds). *Readings in Russian Poetics: Formalist and Structuralist Views*. Cambridge, MA, 1971.

Pomorska, Krystyna. *Russian Formalist Theory and Its Poetic Ambience*. The Hague, 1968.

Propp, Vladimir. *Morphology of the Folktale* [1928], trans. Laurence Scott. Austin, TX, 1968.

Shklovsky, Victor. *A Sentimental Journey: Memoirs, 1917–1922*, trans. Richard Sheldon. Ithaca, NY, 1970.

Shklovsky, Victor. *Theory of prose*, trans. Benjamin Sher. Elmwood Park, 1990.

Steiner, Peter. *Russian Formalism: A Metapoetics*. Ithaca, NY, 1984.

Striedter, Jurij. *Literary Structure, Evolution, and Value: Russian Formalism and Czech Structuralism Reconsidered*. Cambridge, 1989.

Thompson, Ewa M. *Russian Formalism and Anglo-American New Criticism: A Comparative Study*. The Hague, 1971.

Speech Act Theory

Speech act theory has developed from the work of the theoretical school developed by J. L. Austin, author of the influential *How to Do Things with Words* (1962). Speech Act Theory originates from Austin's notion that language eschews conceptions of truth or falsity in favour of larger, more significant claims, particularly ideas about the many ways in which language 'acts' or functions in conversational life. Hence, 'performatives' – or statements that accomplish various acts – do not serve to describe or inform; they involve the action-oriented, first-person present tense, as opposed to the descriptive aspects of the past tense. Subsequently, literary theorists have employed speech act theory as a mechanism for analysing elements of dialogue, narration and linguistic action, while later speech act theorists have also brought to bear philosophical and psychological questions on the condition of utterances. The most 'visible' moment of speech act theory came perhaps following the publication of Jacques Derrida's essay, 'Signature Event Context' ([1971] 1977), which offered an extended critique of Austin's absolute distinction between constative and performative speech acts, which, Derrida argued, became problematised when one took into account matters of iterability and citationality by which all language is marked. Derrida's essay drew a polemical response from John Searle, 'Reiterating the Differences: A Reply to Derrida', to which Derrida subsequently replied in the essay 'Limited Inc abc . . .' (1977).

Bibliography

Austin, J. L. *How to Do Things with Words*. Cambridge, 1962.
Kasher, Asa (ed.). *Pragmatics: Critical Concepts*. London, 1998.
Pratt, Mary Louise. *Towards a Speech Act Theory of Literary Discourse*. Bloomington, IN, 1977.
Searle, John R. *Intentionality: An Essay in the Philosophy of Mind*. Cambridge, 1983.
Searle, John R. *Mind, Language, and Society: Philosophy in the Real World*. New York, 1998.
Tsohatzidis, Savas L. (ed.). *Foundations of Speech Act Theory: Philosophical and Linguistic Perspectives*. London, 1994.

Structuralism

Structuralism refers to the critical methodology that finds its origins in the work of a variety of French literary critics, linguists, anthropologists, psychologists and philosophers during the 1960s, including most significantly Roland Barthes, Gérard Genette and Algirdas Julien Greimas. Many structuralists were influenced by the discoveries of linguist Ferdinand de Saussure, who posited the study of signs as a form of 'semiology' because of its attention to socially and culturally inscribed codes of human interaction. Saussure has had a significant impact on twentieth-century linguistics and literary criticism, particularly his understanding of the verbal sign being composed of two elements, the signifier and the signified. Saussure argues that the fundamental aim of semiotics is to understand the concept of *langue* as a possible result of *parole*. For Saussure, *langue* refers to the basic system of differentiation and combinational rules that allows for a particular usage of signs; *parole* connotes a single verbal utterance, as well as the employment of a sign or set of signs is essential from what is ancillary or accidental. As the smallest basic speech sound or unit of pronunciation, Saussure's ground-breaking conceptualisation of the phoneme represents a signal moment in the history of linguistics. It allows us to distinguish between two different utterances in terms of their measurable physical differences. Saussure explains the relationships between phonemes in terms of their synchronic and diachronic structures. A phoneme exists in a diachronic, or horizontal, relationship with other phonemes that precede and follow it. Synchronic relationships refer to a phoneme's vertical associations with the entire system of language from which individual utterances – or, in regard to the auspices of literary criticism, narratives – derive their meaning. A number of other thinkers participated in the emergence of structuralism, including linguist Roman Jakobson, who conceived of literary works as the result of a series of linguistic structures, Tzvetan Todorov, whose work on the fantastic remains extremely influential, and anthropologist Claude Lévi-Strauss, who was responsible for the widespread dissemination of structuralism as a theoretical concept. Aspects of structuralism were also influential in the work of Louis Althusser, Jacques Lacan and Michel Foucault, and the evidence of indebtedness to structuralism remains today in the various aspects of narratology, as exemplified in the work of Genette.

Bibliography

Barthes, Roland. *Elements of Semiology*, trans. Annette Lavers and Colin Smith. London, 1967.

Barthes, Roland. *Writing Degree Zero*, trans. Annette Lavers and Colin Smith. London, 1967.

Barthes, Roland. *Mythologies*, trans. Annette Lavers. London, 1972.

Barthes, Roland. *S/Z*, trans. by Richard Miller. New York, 1974.

Barthes, Roland. *The Pleasure of the Text*, trans. Richard Miller. London, 1976.

Barthes, Roland. *Image-Music-Text*, ed. and trans. Stephen Heath. Glasgow, 1977.

Barthes, Roland. *Criticism and Truth*, trans. Katherine Pilcher Keuneman. London, 1987.

Culler, Jonathan. *Structuralist Poetics: Structuralism, Linguistics, and the Study of Literature*. London, 1975.

Dosse, François. *History of Structuralism*. 2 Vols. *The Rising Sign, 1945–1966; The Sign Sets, 1967–Present*, trans. Deborah Glassman. Minneapolis, MN, 1997.

Eco, Umberto. *A Theory of Semiotics*. London, 1977.

Ehrmann, Jacques (ed.). *Structuralism*. New York, 1970.

Genette, Gérard. *Narrative Discourse: An Essay on Method*, trans. Jane E. Lewin, foreword Jonathan Culler. Ithaca, NY, 1980.

Genette, Gérard. *The Architext: an Introduction*, trans. Jane E. Lewin. Berkeley, CA, 1992.

Genette, Gérard. *Mimologics*, trans. Thaïs E. Morgan, foreword Gerald Prince. Lincoln, NE, 1995.

Genette, Gérard. *Palimpsests: Literature in the Second Degree*, trans. Channa Newman and Claude Doubinsky, foreword Gerald Prince. Lincoln, NE, 1997.

Genette, Gérard. *Paratexts: Thresholds of Interpretation*, trans. Jane E. Lewin, foreword Richard Macksey. Cambridge, 1997.

Greimas, A. J. *Structural Semantics: An Attempt at a Method*, trans. Daniele McDowell, Ronald Schleifer and Alan Velie, intro. Ronald Schleifer. Lincoln, NE, 1983.

Greimas, A. J. *On Meaning: Selected Writings in Semiotic Theory*, trans. Paul Perron and Frank Collins, foreword Fredric Jameson, intro. Paul Perron. Minneapolis, MN, 1987.

Greimas, A. J. *Narrative Semiotics and Cognitive Discourses*, foreword Paolo Fabbri and Paul Perron, trans. Paul Perron and Frank H. Collins. London, 1990.

Hawkes, Terence. *Structuralism and Criticism*. London, 1977.

Jakobson, Roman. *Selected Writings*. The Hague, 1962.

Jakobson, Roman. *The Framework of Language*. Ann Arbor, MI, 1980.

Jakobson, Roman. *Language in Literature*, ed. and intro. Krystyna Pomorska and Stephen Rudy. Cambridge, MA, 1989.

Jakobson, Roman and Morris Halle. *Fundamentals of Language*. The Hague, 1956.

Jameson, Fredric. *The Prison-House of Language: A Critical Account of Structuralism and Russian Formalism*. Princeton, NJ, 1972.

Lane, Michael (ed.). *Structuralism: A Reader*. London, 1970.

Lévi-Strauss, Claude. *Tristes Tropiques*. New York, 1961.

Lévi-Strauss, Claude. *The Elementary Structures of Kinship*, trans. James Harle Bell et al., ed. Rodney Needham. Boston, 1969.

Lévi-Strauss, Claude. *The Raw and the Cooked*, trans. John and Doreen Weightman. New York, 1969.

Lévi-Strauss, Claude. *From Honey to Ashes*, trans. John and Doreen Weightman. New York, 1973.

Lévi-Strauss, Claude. *Anthropology and Myth: Lectures 1951–1982*, trans. Roy Wills. Oxford, 1987.

Lotman, Yuri. *The Structure of the Artistic Text*. Ann Arbor, MI, 1977.

Macksey, Richard with Eugenio Donato (eds). *The Structuralist Controversy: The Languages of Criticism and the Sciences of Man*. Baltimore, MD, 1972.

Robey, David (ed.). *Structuralism: An Introduction*. Oxford, 1973.

Saussure, Ferdinand de. *Course in General Linguistics*, trans. Wade Baskin. London, 1978.

Scholes, Robert E. *Structuralism in Literature: An Introduction*. New Haven, CT, 1974.

Todorov, Tzvetan. *The Fantastic: A Structural Approach to a Literary Genre*, trans. Richard Howard. Ithaca, NY, 1975.

Todorov, Tzvetan. *Introduction to Poetics*, trans. Richard Howard. Minneapolis, MN, 1981.

Todorov, Tzvetan. *The Poetics of Prose,* trans. Richard Howard. Brighton, 1981.

Textual Criticism

Textual criticism refers to the discipline – frequently associated with bibliographical study – that addresses the transmission of texts, editorial theory and the study of textual variants. Often drawing upon many of the insights produced by analytical and descriptive bibliography, textual critics attempt to provide readers with explanations for alterations and variations that occur during a given book's textual production. Textual criticism's signal moment in the twentieth century involves W. W. Greg's important essay on 'The Rationale of Copy-Text', in which Greg locates textual authority with the first edition of a text in the absence of revision in a later edition. Greg, R. B. McKerrow and A. W. Pollard established what came to be known as the 'New Bibliography', a movement that championed the text as a physical object and emphasised the study of the technical aspects of book production.

Bibliography

Baker, William and Kenneth Womack. *Twentieth-Century Bibliography and Textual Criticism: An Annotated Bibliography*. Westport, CT, 2000.

Bowers, Fredson. *Bibliography and Textual Criticism*. Oxford, 1964.

Bowers, Fredson. *Essays in Bibliography, Text, and Editing*. Charlottesville, VA, 1975.

Bowers, Fredson. *Principles of Bibliographical Description*. New Castle, 1995.

Gaskell, Philip. *A New Introduction to Bibliography*. Oxford, 1972.

Gaskell, Philip. *From Writer to Readers: Studies in Editorial Method*. Oxford, 1978.

Greetham, D. C. *Textual Scholarship: An Introduction* [1992]. New York, 1994.

Greg, W. W. *Collected Papers*, ed. J. C. Maxwell. Oxford, 1966.

McGann, Jerome J. *The Textual Condition*. Princeton, NJ, 1991.

McGann, Jerome J. *A Critique of Modern Textual Criticism* [1983]. Chicago, 1992.

McKenzie, D. F. *Bibliography and the Sociology of Texts*. London, 1986.

McKerrow, Ronald B. *An Introduction to Bibliography for Literary Students*. Oxford, 1928; New Castle, 1995.

Parker, Hershel. *Flawed Texts and Verbal Icons: Literary Authority in American Fiction*. Evanston, IL, 1984.

Shillingsburg, Peter L. *Scholarly Editing in the Computer Age: Theory and Practice*, 3rd edn. Athens, OH, 1996.

Shillingsburg, Peter L. *Resisting Texts: Authority and Submission in Constructions of Meaning*. Ann Arbor, MI, 1998.

Tanselle, G. Thomas. *Textual Criticism since Greg: A Chronicle, 1950–1985*. Charlottesville, VA, 1988.

Tanselle, G. Thomas. *A Rationale of Textual Criticism*. Philadelphia, 1989.

Tanselle, G. Thomas. *Literature and Artifacts*. Charlottesville, VA, 1998.

Thorpe, James. *Principles of Textual Criticism*. San Marino, 1972.

Williams, William P. and Craig S. Abbott. *An Introduction to Bibliographical and Textual Studies*, 3rd edn. New York, 1999.

Chronology of Critical Thinkers, with Bibliographies

The following chronology provides, along with dates of subjects, key publications, which consist either of major works or well-established collections such as 'readers'; where these publications were originally in a language other than English, translations are given for reasons of student accessibility. Dates of publication reflect publication of translation, where applicable, rather than original date of publication. Neither the chronology nor the bibliographies appended are intended to be exhaustive but, rather, are suggested as indicative of key influences persistent within various aspects of literary criticism and related disciplinary areas of study.

Immanuel Kant (1724–1804)

The Critique of Judgement, trans. James Creed Meredith. Oxford, 1952.
Critique of Pure Reason, trans. Paul Guyer and Allen W. Wood. Cambridge, 1998.
The Metaphysics of Morals, trans. Mary Gregor. Cambridge, 1996.

Georg Wilhelm Friedrich Hegel (1770–1830)

Introductory Lectures on Aesthetics, trans. Bernard Bosanquet. London, 1993.
Phenomenology of Spirit, trans. J. M. Findlay. Oxford, 1979.
Philosophy of Right, trans. T. M. Knox. New York, 1968.

William Hazlitt (1778–1830)

Fight and Other Writings, ed. David Chandler. London, 2000.
Metropolitan Writings, ed. Gregory Dart. London, 2005.

Samuel Taylor Coleridge (1782–1834)

Biographia Literaria, ed. Nigel Leask. London, 1997.

Arthur Schopenhauer (1788–1860)

Essays and Aphorisms, ed. R. J. Hollingdale. London, 2004.
World as Will and Idea, trans. Jill Berman. Ed. David Berman. London, 2004.
The World as Will and Representation vols I & II, trans. E. F. J. Payne. New York, 1967.

Søren Kierkegaard (1813–1855)

Either/Or: A Fragment of Life, trans. Alistair Hannay, ed. Victor Eremita. London, 1992.
Fear and Trembling, trans. Alistair Hannay. London, 1985.
The Sickness unto Death, trans. Alistair Hannay. Harmondsworth, 1989.

Karl Marx (1818–1883)

Capital, Vols 1–3, trans. Ben Fowkes (vol. 1); David Fernbach (vols 2 and 3), int. Ernest Mandel. London, 1990–92.
(with Friedrich Engels). *The Communist Manifesto*, intro. A. J. P. Taylor. London, 1985.
(with Friedrich Engels). *The German Ideology: Students Edition*, ed. and intro. C. J. Arthur. London, 1970.
Grundrisse, trans. Martin Nicolaus. London, 1993.
Selected Writings, ed. David McLellan. Oxford, 1977.

John Ruskin (1819–1900)

Praeterita, ed. Timothy Hilton. London, 2005.
Selected Writings, ed. Dinah Birch. Oxford, 2004.
Unto this Last and Other Writings, ed. Clive Wilmer. London, 1985.

Matthew Arnold (1822–1888)

Culture and Anarchy, ed. Samuel Lipman. New Haven, CT, 1994.
Selected Prose, ed. P. J. Keating. London, 1987.

Walter Pater (1839–1894)

The Renaissance: Studies in Art and Poetry, ed. Adam Phillips. Oxford, 1986.

Charles Sanders Peirce (1839–1914)

Peirce on Signs: Writings on Semiotic, ed. James Hoopes. Chapel Hill, NC, 1991.

Friedrich Nietzsche (1844–1900)

Beyond Good and Evil: Prelude to a Philosophy of the Future, trans. and intro. R. J. Hollingdale. London, 1973.

The Birth of Tragedy: Out of the Spirit of Music, trans. Shaun Whiteside, intro. Michael Tanner. London, 1994.

Ecce Homo: How One Becomes What One Is, trans. and intro. R. J. Hollingdale. London, 1979.

Thus Spake Zarathustra: A Book for Everyone and No-one, trans. and intro. R. J. Hollingdale. London, 1969.

Twilight of the Idols/The Anti-Christ, trans. and intro. R. J. Hollingdale. London, 1968.

Sigmund Freud (1856–1939)

The Interpretation of Dreams. Penguin Freud Library, Vol. 4, trans. James Strachey, eds. James Strachey, Alan Tyson and Angela Richards. London, 1991.

Introductory Lectures on Psychoanalysis. Penguin Freud Library, Vol. 1 trans. James Strachey, eds. James Strachey and Angela Richards. London, 1982.

The Psychopathology of Everyday Life. Penguin Freud Library, Vol. 5, trans. Alan Tyson, eds. James Strachey, Alan Tyson and Angela Richards. London, 1991.

On Sexuality, Penguin Freud Library, Vol. 7, trans. James Strachey, ed. Angela Richards. London, 1991.

Writings on Art and Literature, trans. James Strachey et al., foreword Neil Hertz. Stanford, CA, 1997.

Ferdinand de Saussure (1857–1913)

Course in General Linguistics, trans. Wade Baskin. New York, 1959.

Edmund Husserl (1859–1938)

Cartesian Meditations: An Introduction to Phenomenology, trans. Dorion Cairns. The Hague, 1960.

The Crisis of European Sciences and Transcendental Phenomenology: An Introduction to Phenomenological Philosophy, trans. David Carr. Evanston, IL, 1970.

The Idea of Phenomenology, trans. William P. Alston and George Nakhnikian. Dordrecht, 1964.

On the Phenomenology of the Consciousness of Internal Time, trans. John Barnett Brough. Dordrecht, 1991.

Phenomenology and the Crisis of Philosophy: Philosophy as Rigorous Science, and, Philosophy and the Crisis of European Man, trans. Quentin Lauer. New York, 1965.

Carl Gustav Jung (1875–1961)

The Development of Personality. London, 1991.
Man and his Symbols. New York, 1964.
Psychology and the East. London, 1986.

Gaston Bachelard (1884–1962)

The Philosophy of No: A Philosophy of the New Scientific Mind. Trans. G.C. Waterson. New York, 1968.
The Poetics of Space, trans. Maria Jolas. Boston, 1994.

György Lukács (1885–1971)

Essays on Realism, trans. David Fernbach, ed. Rodney Livingstone. Cambridge, MA, 1981.

The Historical Novel, trans. Hannah and Stanley Mitchell. Lincoln, NE, 1983.

Studies in European Realism: A Sociological Survey of the Writings of Balzac, Stendhal, Zola, Tolstoy, Gorki and Others, trans. Edith Bone. London, 1950.

The Theory of the Novel: A Historico-Philosophical Essay on the Forms of Great Epic Literature, trans. Anna Bostock. Cambridge, MA, 1971.

Writer & Critic and Other Essays, trans. Arthur D. Kahn. New York, 1970.

R. S. Crane (1886–1967)

Critical and Historical Principles of Literary History. Chicago, 1971.
The Idea of the Humanities and Other Essays Critical and Historical, 2 vols. Chicago, 1967.
The Languages of Criticism and the Structure of Poetry. Toronto, 1953.

T. S. Eliot (1888–1965)

To Criticize the Critic and Other Writings. London, 1965.
The Sacred Wood: Essays on Poetry and Criticism. London, 1960.
Selected Essays. London, 1951.
The Use of Poetry and the Use of Criticism. London, 1933.

John Crowe Ransom (1888–1974)

The New Criticism. Norfolk, VA, 1941.

Martin Heidegger (1889–1976)

Being and Time, trans. Joan Stambaugh. Albany, NY, 1996.
An Introduction to Metaphysics, trans. Ralph Manheim. New Haven, CT, 1959.
Poetry, Language, Thought, trans. Albert Hofstadter. New York, 1971.
On the Way to Language, trans. Peter D. Hertz. San Francisco, 1982.
What is Called Thinking?, trans. J. Glenn Gray. New York, 1968.

Ludwig Wittgenstein (1889–1951)

The Blue and Brown Books: Preliminary Studies for the Philosophical Investigations, trans. G. E. M. Anscombe. Oxford, 1958.
Culture and Value, trans. Peter Winch. Oxford, 1997.
Philosophical Investigations, trans. G. E. M. Anscombe. Oxford, 1973.
Tractatus Logico-Philosophicus, trans. D. F. Pears and B. F. McGuinness, intro. Bertrand Russell. London, 1974.

Antonio Gramsci (1891–1937)

Prison Notebooks. Vols 1 and 2, trans. and ed. Joseph Buttigieg. New York, 1992.
Selections from the Cultural Writings, eds David Forgacs and Geoffrey Nowell Smith. London, 1985.

Selections from Political Writings, 1910–1920, ed. Quintin Hoare. London, 1977.
Selections from Political Writings, 1921–1926, ed. Quintin Hoare. London, 1978.

Jan Mukarovsky (1891–1975)

On Poetic Language. New York, 1976.

Erich Auerbach (1892–1957)

Literary Language and its Public in Late Latin Antiquity and in the Middle Ages, foreword Jan M. Ziolkowski, trans. Ralph Manheim. Princeton, NJ, 1993.
Mimesis: The Representation of Reality in Western Literature, intro. Edward W. Said, trans. W. R. Trask. Princeton, NJ, 2003.

Walter Benjamin (1892–1940)

Illuminations, ed. and intro. Hannah Arendt, trans. Harry Zohn. London, 1970.
One Way Street and Other Writings, trans. Edmund Jephcott and Kingsley Shorter. London, 1979.
Reflections: Essays, Aphorisms, Autobiographical Writings, trans. Edmund Jephcott, ed. and intro. Peter Demetz. New York, 1978.
Selected Writings Vol 1: 1913–1926, eds. Marcus Bullock and Michael W. Jennings. Cambridge, MA, 1996.
Selected Writings Vol. 2: 1927–1934, eds. Michael W. Jennings et al. Cambridge, MA, 1999.
Understanding Brecht, trans. Anna Bostock, intro. Stanley Mitchell. London, 1977.

Roman Ingarden (1893–1970)

The Cognition of the Literary Work of Art, trans. Ruth Ann Crowley and Kenneth R. Olson. Evanston, IL, 1973.
The Literary Work of Art: An Investigation on the Borderline of Ontology, Logic and Theory of Literature. Trans. George G. Grabowicz. Evanston, IL, 1973.
The Ontology of the Work of Art: The Musical Work, the Picture, the Architectural Work, the Film, trans. Raymond Meyer and John T. Goldthwait. Athens, OH, 1989.

I. A. Richards (1893–1979)

Coleridge on Imagination, 3rd edn. London, 1962.
Poetries and Sciences, orig. pub. *Science and Poetry*. New York, 1970.
Practical Criticism: A Study of Literary Judgement. London, 1964.
Principles of Literary Criticism. London, 1960.

Victor Shklovsky (1893–1984)

Theory of Prose, trans. Benjamin Sher. Elmwood Park, 1990.

Mikhail Bakhtin (1895–1975)

Art and Answerability: Early Philosophical Essays by M. M. Bakhtin,
    eds. Michael Holquist and Vadim Liapunov, trans. Vadim Liapunov.
    Austin, TX, 1990.
The Dialogic Imagination: Four Essays, ed. Michael Holquist, trans.
    Caryl Emerson and Michael Holquist. Austin, TX, 1981.
Problems of Dostoevsky's Poetics, ed. and trans. Caryl Emerson. Min-
    neapolis, MN, 1984.
Rabelais and His World, Trans. Hélène Iswolsky. Cambridge, MA,
    1968.
Speech Genres and Other Late Essays, eds. Caryl Emerson and Michael
    Holquist, trans. Vern W. McGee. Austin, TX, 1986.

Vladimir Propp (1895–1970)

Morphology of the Folk Tale, trans. Laurence Stott, intro. Svatava
    Pirkova-Jakobson. Austin, TX, 1968.
Theory and History of Folklore, trans. Ariadna Y. Martin and Richard P.
    Martin, ed. and intro. Anatoly Liberman. Minneapolis, MN, 1984.

Max Horkheimer (1895–1973)

(with Theodor Adorno). *Dialectic of Enlightenment*, trans. John Cum-
    ming. London, 1979.

F. R. Leavis (1895–1978)

The Common Pursuit. London, 1952.
English Literature in Our Time and the University. London, 1969.
The Great Tradition: George Eliot, Henry James, Joseph Conrad.
    London, 1948.

The Living Principle: 'English' as a Discipline of Thought. London, 1975.

New Bearings in English Poetry. London, 1932.

Roman Jakobson (1896–1982)

The Framework of Language. Ann Arbor, MI, 1980.

(with Morris Halle). *Fundamentals of Language*. The Hague, 1956.

Language in Literature, eds. and intro. Krystyna Pomorska and Stephen Rudy. Cambridge, MA, 1989.

Selected Writings. The Hague, 1962.

Georges Bataille (1897–1962)

The Accursed Share, 3 vols, trans. Robert Hurley. New York, 1989.

Guilty, trans. Bruce Boone. New York, 1988.

The Impossible, trans. Robert Hurley. San Francisco, 1991.

Inner Experience, trans. Leslie Anne Boldt. Albany, NY, 1988.

Visions of Excess: Selected Writings, 1927–1939, ed. Allan Stoekl, trans. Allan Stoekl, with Carl R. Lovitts and Donald M. Leslie, Jr. Minneapolis, MN, 1989.

Bertolt Brecht (1898–1956)

Brecht on Film and Radio, trans. and ed. Marc Silberman. London, 2000.

Brecht on Theatre: The Development of an Aesthetic, trans. and ed. John Willett. New York, 1964.

Herbert Marcuse (1898–1979)

The Aesthetic Dimension: Toward a Critique of Marxist Aesthetics. Boston, 1979.

Eros and Civilisation: A Philosophical Inquiry into Freud. Boston, 1955.

Five Lectures: Psychoanalysis, Politics, and Utopia, trans. Jeremy J. Shapiro and Shierry M. Weber. Boston, 1970.

Negations: Essays in Critical Theory, trans. Jeremy J. Shapiro. Boston, 1968.

One Dimensional Man: Studies in the Ideology of Advanced Industrial Society, trans. Jeremy J. Shapiro. London, 1968.

Hans-Georg Gadamer (1900–2002)

Gadamer on Celan: 'Who am I and Who are You?' and Other Essays, trans. and eds. Richard Heinemann and Bruce Krajewski. Albany, NY, 1997.
The Relevance of the Beautiful and Other Essays, trans. Nicholas Walker, ed. Robert Bernasconi. Cambridge, 1986.
Truth and Method, trans. rev. Joel Weinsheimer and Donald G. Marshall. 2nd edn. London, 1989.

Jacques Lacan (1901–1981)

The Four Fundamental Concepts of Psycho-Analysis, trans. Alan Sheridan, ed. Jacques-Alain Miller, intro. David Macey. London, 1994.
Écrits: A Selection, trans. Alan Sheridan. New York, 1977.
(with the école freudienne) *Feminine Sexuality*, eds. Juliet Mitchell and Jacqueline Rose, trans. Jacqueline Rose. New York, 1982.
Speech and Language in Psychoanalysis, trans. Anthony Wilden. Baltimore, MD, 1968.
Television: A Challenge to the Psychoanalytic Establishment, trans. Denis Hollier, Rosalind Krauss and Annette Michelson, ed. Joan Copjec. New York, 1990.

Fernand Braudel (1902–1985)

Civilization and Capitalism, 15th–18th Century, 3 vols. London, 2002.
The Mediterranean in the Ancient World, trans. Sian Reynolds, intro. Oswyn Murray. London, 2002.
On History, trans. Sarah Matthews. Chicago, IL, 1982.

Theodor W. Adorno (1903–1969)

Aesthetic Theory, trans. Robert Hullot-Kentor. Minneapolis, MN, 1970.
Minima Moralia: Reflections on Damaged Life, trans. E. F. N. Jephcott. London, 1974.
Negative Dialectics, trans. E. B. Ashton. London, 1973.
Prisms, trans. Samuel and Shierry Weber. London, 1967.

René Wellek (1903–1995)

Discriminations: Further Concepts of Criticism. New Haven, CT, 1970.
Four Critics: Croce, Valéry, Lukacs and Ingarden. Seattle, WA, 1982.
(with Austen Warren) *Theory of Literature*. Harmondsworth, 1987.

Georges Canguilhem (1904–1995)

Ideology and Rationality in the History of the Life Sciences. Cambridge, MA, 1988.
The Normal and the Pathological. New York, 1991.
Delaporte, F. (ed.). *A Vital Rationalist: Selected Writings from Georges Canguilhem.* New York, 1994.

Jean-Paul Sartre (1905–1980)

Being and Nothingness: An Essay on Phenomenological Ontology, trans. E. Barnes. London, 1957.
Between Existentialism and Marxism, trans. John Mathews. New York, 1975.
Critique of Dialectical Reason. 1, Theory of Practical Ensembles, trans. Alan Sheridan-Smith, ed. Jonathan Ree. London, 1976.
Essays in Aesthetics. New York, 1963.
'What is Literature?' and Other Essays. Cambridge, MA, 1988.

Lionel Trilling (1905–1975)

Beyond Culture: Essays on Literature and Learning. Harmondsworth, 1967.
The Moral Obligation to be Intelligent: Selected Essays, ed. Leon Wieseltier. New York, 2001.
Sincerity and Authenticity. Cambridge, MA, 1974.

Hannah Arendt (1906–1975)

Eichmann in Jerusalem: A Report on the Banality of Evil. London, 1994.
On Revolution. London, 1991.
The Origins of Totalitarianism. New York, 1973.

William Empson (1906–1984)

Argufying: Essays on Literature and Culture, ed. John Haffenden. London, 1981.
Milton's God. Cambridge, 1981.
Seven Types of Ambiguity. Harmondsworth, 1961.
Some Versions of Pastoral. Harmondsworth, 1965.
The Structure of Complex Words. London, 1951.

Emmanuel Levinas (1906–1995)

Basic Philosophical Writings, eds. Adriaan T. Peperzak, Simon Critchley, and Robert Bernasconi. Bloomington, IN, 1996.
The Levinas Reader, ed. Seán Hand. Oxford, 1989.
Otherwise than Being or, Beyond Essence, trans. Richard A. Cohen. Pittsburgh, PA, 1998.
Time and the Other, trans. Richard A. Cohen. Pittsburgh, PA, 1987.
Totality and Infinity: An Essay on Exteriority, trans. Alphonso Lingis. Pittsburgh, PA, 1969.

Cleanth Brooks (1906–1994)

An Approach to Literature. New York, 1939.
Historical Evidence and the Reading of Seventeenth-Century Poetry. Columbia, OH, 1991.
Modern Poetry and the Tradition. Chapel Hill, NC, 1939.
(with Robert Penn Warren). *Understanding Poetry*, 2nd edn. New York, 1950.
The Well Wrought Urn: Studies in the Structure of Poetry. New York, 1947.

Maurice Blanchot (1907–2003)

The Blanchot Reader, ed. George Quasha. New York, 1999.
Friendship, trans. Elizabeth Rottenberg. Stanford, CA, 1997.
The Infinite Conversation, trans. Susan Hanson. Minneapolis, MN, 1993.
The Space of Literature, trans. Ann Smock. Lincoln, NE, 1982.
The Writing of the Disaster, trans. Ann Smock. Lincoln, NE, 1986.

W. K. Wimsatt (1907–1975)

Hateful Contraries: Studies in Literature and Criticism. Lexington, 1965.
Literary Criticism. New York, 1957.
The Verbal Icon: Studies in the Meaning of Poetry. Lexington, 1954.

Simone de Beauvoir (1908–1986)

Brigitte Bardot and the Lolita Syndrome, foreword George Amberg. New York, 1972.
The Ethics of Ambiguity, trans. Bernard Frechtman. New York, 1948.
The Long March, trans. Austryn Wainhouse. Cleveland, OH, 1958.
The Second Sex, trans. and ed. H. M. Parshley, intro. Margaret Crosland. New York, 1993.

Claude Lévi-Strauss (1908–)

Anthropology and Myth: Lectures 1951–1982, trans. Roy Wills. Oxford, 1987.
The Elementary Structures of Kinship, trans. James Harle Bell et al., ed. Rodney Needham. Boston, 1969.
From Honey to Ashes., trans. John and Doreen Weightman. New York, 1973.
The Raw and the Cooked, trans. John and Doreen Weightman. New York, 1969.
Tristes Tropiques. New York, 1961.

Maurice Merleau-Ponty (1908–1961)

The Merleau-Ponty Aesthetics Reader: Philosophy and Painting, ed. and intro. Galen A. Johnson, trans. Michael B. Smith. Evanston, IL, 1993.
Phenomenology of Perception, trans. Colin Smith. London, 1962.
The Prose of the World, ed. Claude Lefort, trans. John O'Neill. Evanston, IL, 1973.
The Visible and the Invisible, ed. Claude Lefort, trans. Alphonso Lingis. Evanston, IL, 1968.

J. L. Austin (1911–1960)

How to Do Things With Words, 2nd edn. Cambridge, MA, 1975.
Philosophical Papers, 3rd edn. Oxford, 1979.
Sense and Sensibilia. New York, 1964.

M. H. Abrams (1912–)

Doing Things with Texts: Essays in Criticism and Critical Theory. New York, 1989.
The Mirror and the Lamp: Romantic Theory and the Critical Tradition. New York, 1965.
Natural Supernaturalism: Tradition and Revolution in Romantic Literature. New York, 1973.

Northrop Frye (1912–1991)

Anatomy of Criticism: Four Essays. Princeton, NJ, 1957.
The Critical Path: An Essay on the Social Context of Literary Criticism. Bloomington, IN, 1971.
Fables of Identity: Studies in Poetic Mythology. New York, 1963.

Fearful Symmetry: A Study of William Blake. Princeton, NJ, 1947.
The Stubborn Structure: Essays on Criticism and Society. Ithaca, NY, 1970.

Paul Ricœur (1913–2005)

The Conflict of Interpretations: Essays in Hermeneutics. London, 1989.
Critique and Conviction, trans. K. Blamey. Cambridge, 1997.
Hermeneutics and the Human Sciences: Essays on Language, Action and Interpretation, ed. and trans. J. Thompson. Cambridge, 1981.
The Rule of Metaphor: Multi-Disciplinary Studies of the Creation of Meaning in Language, trans. R. Czerny et al. London, 1978.
From Text to Action: Essays in Hermeneutics II, trans. K. Blamey. London, 1991.

Roland Barthes (1915–1980)

Image-Music-Text, ed. and trans. Stephen Heath. Glasgow, 1977.
Mythologies, ed. and trans. Annette Lavers. London, 1973.
The Pleasure of the Text, trans. Richard Miller. New York, 1975.
S/Z, trans. by Richard Miller. New York, 1974
Writing Degree Zero, trans. Annette Lavers and Colin Smith. New York, 1967.

A. J. Greimas (1917–1992)

On Meaning: Selected Writings in Semiotic Theory, trans. Paul Perron and Frank Collins, foreword Fredric Jameson, intro. Paul Perron. Minneapolis, MN, 1987.
Narrative Semiotics and Cognitive Discourses, foreword Paolo Fabbri and Paul Perron, trans. Paul Perron and Frank H. Collins. London, 1990.
Structural Semantics: An Attempt at a Method, trans. Daniele McDowell, Ronald Schleifer and Alan Velie, intro. Ronald Schleifer. Lincoln, NE, 1983.

Eric Hobsbawm (1917–)

The Age of Capital, 1848–1875. London, 1988.
The Age of Empire, 1875–1914. London, 1989.
Industry and Empire: From 1750 to the Present Day. London, 1999.

Ian Watt (1917–1999)

The Rise of The Novel: Studies in Defoe, Richardson and Fielding. London, 1957.

Louis Althusser (1918–1990)

Lenin and Philosophy, trans. Ben Brewster. London, 1971.
For Marx, trans. Ben Brewster. London, 1977.
Philosophy and the Spontaneous Philosophy of the Scientists, trans. Ben Brewster et al., Gregory Elliot. Ed. and intro. London, 1990.
(with Etienne Balibar). *Reading Capital*, trans. Ben Brewster. London, 1970.

Richard Ellmann (1918–1987)

Four Dubliners. New York, 1988.
James Joyce. Oxford, 1959.
Oscar Wilde. Oxford, 1988.
Ulysses on the Liffey. Oxford, 1972.
Yeats: The Man and the Masks. London, 1948.

Richard Hoggart (1918–)

The Uses of Literacy. London, 1958.

Frank Kermode (1919–)

The Art of Telling: Essays on Fiction. Cambridge, MA, 1983.
The Classic: Literary Images of Permanence and Change. Cambridge, MA, 1983.
The Genesis of Secrecy: On the Interpretation of Narrative. Cambridge, MA, 1979.
The Sense of an Ending: Studies in the Theory of Fiction. Oxford, 1968.
The Uses of Error. Cambridge, MA, 1991.

Paul de Man (1919–1983)

Aesthetic Ideology, ed. and intro. Andrzej Warminski. Minneapolis, MN, 1996.
Allegories of Reading: Figural Language in Rousseau, Nietzsche, Rilke, and Proust. New Haven, 1979.
Blindness and Insight: Essays in the Rhetoric of Contemporary Criticism, 2nd ed. Wlad Godzich. Minneapolis, MN, 1983.

The Resistance to Theory, foreword Wlad Godzich. Minneapolis, MN, 1986.
The Rhetoric of Romanticism. New York, 1984.

Wayne C. Booth (1921–)

The Rhetoric of Fiction. Chicago, 1961.
A Rhetoric of Irony. Chicago, 1974.

Raymond Williams (1921–1988)

The Country and the City. New York, 1973.
Culture and Society 1780–1950. Harmondsworth, 1963.
The English Novel: From Dickens to Lawrence. St Albans, 1974.
The Long Revolution. Harmondsworth, 1965.
Marxism and Literature. Oxford, 1977.

René Girard (1923–)

The Scapegoat, trans. Y. Freccero. Baltimore, MD, 1986.
*To Double Business Bound: Essays on Literature, Mimesis and Anthro-
    pology*. Baltimore, MD, 1988.
Violence and the Sacred. London, 2005.

Paul Feyerabend (1924–1994)

Against Method: Outline of an Anarchistic Theory of Knowledge.
    London, 1993.
Farewell to Reason. London, 1987.
Three Dialogues on Knowledge. Oxford, 1991.

E. P. Thompson (1924–1993)

Making History: Writings on History and Culture. London, 1995.
The Making of the English Working Class. London, 1991.
Witness Against the Beast: William Blake and the Moral Law, foreword
    Christopher Hill. Cambridge, 1994.

Zygmunt Bauman (1925–)

Identity. Oxford, 2004.
Modernity and Ambivalence. Ithaca, NY, 1991.
Postmodern Ethics. Oxford, 1993.

Michel de Certeau (1925–1986)

The Capture of Speech and Other Political Writing, trans. Tom Conley. Minneapolis, 1997.
Culture in the Plural, trans. Tom Conley. Minneapolis, MN, 1994.
Heterologies: Discourse on the Other, trans. Brian Massumi. Minneapolis, MN, 1986.
The Practice of Everyday Life, trans. Steven Rendall. Berkeley, CA, 1984.
The Writing of History, trans. Tom Conley. New York, 1988.

Gilles Deleuze (1925–1995)

Difference and Repetition, trans. Paul Patton. New York, 1994.
Essays: Critical and Clinical, trans. Daniel W. Smith and Michael A. Greco. Minneapolis, MN, 1997.
(with Félix Guattari). *Kafka: Toward a Minor Literature*, trans. Dana Polan. Minneapolis, MA, 1986.
Negotiations: 1972–1990, trans. Martin Joughin. New York, 1995.
(with Félix Guattari). *Nomadology: The War Machine*, trans. Brian Massumi. New York, 1986.

Frantz Fanon (1925–1961)

Black Skin, White Masks. New York, 1967.
The Wretched of the Earth. New York, 1968.

Jean-François Lyotard (1925–1998)

The Differend: Phrases in Dispute, trans. George Van Den Abeele. Manchester, 1988.
The Inhuman: Reflections on Time, trans. Geoffrey Bennington and Rachel Bowlby. Cambridge, 1991.
Just Gaming, trans. Wlad Godzich. Manchester, 1985.
Libidinal Economy, trans. Iain Hamilton Grant. London, 1993.
The Postmodern Condition: a Report on Knowledge, trans. Geoff Bennington and Brian Massumi. Manchester, 1985.

John Berger (1926–)

About Looking. London, 1992.
The Sense of Sight. London, 1993.
Ways of Seeing. London, 1990.

Michel Foucault (1926–1984)

The Archaeology of Knowledge, trans. A. M. Sheridan-Smith. London, 1972.
The Birth of the Clinic: An Archaeology of Medical Perception, trans. A. M. Sheridan-Smith. New York, 1975.
Discipline and Punish: The Birth of the Prison, trans. Alan Sheridan. London, 1977.
The History of Sexuality, Vol. I: An Introduction, trans. Robert Hurley. London, 1979.
Madness and Civilization: A History of Insanity in the Age of Reason, trans. Richard Howard. London, 1967.

Wolfgang Iser (1926–)

The Act of Reading: A Theory of Aesthetic Response. London, 1978.
The Implied Reader: Patterns of Communication in Prose Fiction from Bunyan to Beckett. Baltimore, MD, 1974.
Prospecting: from Reader Response to Literary Anthropology. Baltimore, 1989.

Norman Holland (1927–)

The Dynamics of Literary Response. New York, 1968.
5 Readers Reading. New Haven, CT, 1975.
Poems in Persons: An Introduction to the Psychoanalysis of Literature. New York, 1973.

Noam Chomsky (1928–)

Aspects of the Theory of Syntax. Cambridge, MA, 1965.
Language and Politics. Montreal, 1989.
Language and Responsibility. New York, 1979.

J. Hillis Miller (1928–)

The Ethics of Reading: Kant, de Man, Eliot, Trollope, James, and Benjamin. New York, 1987.
Charles Dickens: The World of His Novels. Cambridge, MA, 1958.
The Disappearance of God: Five Nineteenth-Century Writers. New York, 1965.
Fiction and Repetition: Seven English Novels. Cambridge, MA, 1982.
Topographies. Stanford, CA, 1995.

Hayden White (1928–)

*The Content of the Form: Narrative Discourse and Historical Repre-
sentation.* Baltimore, MD, 1990.
Metahistory: The Historical Imagination in Nineteenth-Century Europe.
Baltimore, MD, 1975.
Tropics of Discourse: Essays in Cultural Criticism. Baltimore, MD, 1985.

Jean Baudrillard (1929–)

Fatal Strategies, trans. Philip Beitchman and W. G. J. Niesluchowski.
New York, 1990.
The Illusion of the End, trans. Chris Turner. Stanford, CA, 1994.
The Mirror of Production, trans. Mark Poster. St Louis, MO, 1975.
Selected Writings, ed. and intro. Mark Poster. Stanford, 1988.
The System of Objects, trans. James Benedict. London, 1996.

Harold Bloom (1929–)

The Anxiety of Influence: A Theory of Poetry. Oxford, 1973.
(with Paul de Man, Jacques Derrida, Geoffrey Hartman and J. Hillis
Miller). *Deconstruction and Criticism.* New York, 1979.
A Map of Misreading. Oxford, 1975.
Omens of the Millenium. London, 1997.
The Visionary Company: A Reading of English Romantic Poetry, revised
and enlarged edn. Ithaca, NY 1971.

Jürgen Habermas (1929–)

Autonomy and Solidarity, ed. Peter Dews. London, 1992.
Jürgen Habermas on Society and Politics, ed. Steven Seidman. Boston,
1989.
Knowledge and Human Interests, trans. Jeremy J. Shapiro. Boston,
1971.
The Philosophical Discourse of Modernity, trans. Frederick Lawrence.
Cambridge, MA, 1990.
*Theory of Communicative Action. Vol. 1: Reason and the Rationaliza-
tion of Society,* trans. Thomas McCarthy. Boston, 1984.

Geoffrey Hartman (1929–)

Beyond Formalism: Literary essays 1958–1970. New Haven, CT, 1970.
The Fateful Question of Culture. New York, 1997.

Saving the Text: Literature, Derrida, Philosophy. Baltimore, MD, 1981.
The Unmediated Vision: An Interpretation of Wordsworth, Hopkins, Rilke, and Valéry. New Haven, CT, 1954.
Wordsworth's Poetry 1787–1814, 2nd edn. with a new essay. New Haven, CT, 1971.

George Steiner (1929–)

After Babel: Aspects of Language and Translation. Oxford, 1998.
The Death of Tragedy. London, 1996.
George Steiner: A Reader. Oxford, 1987.

Pierre Bourdieu (1930–2002)

Bourdieu: On Television and Journalism. London, 1998.
Distinction: A Social Critique of the Judgment of Taste, trans. Richard Nice. Cambridge, MA, 1984.
The Field of Cultural Production: Essays on Art and Literature, ed. and intro. R. Johnson. New York, 1993.
Photography, trans. Shaun Whiteside. Oxford, 1996.
The Rules of Art: Genesis and Structure in the Literary Field, trans. Susan Emanuel. Stanford, CA, 1995.

Jacques Derrida (1930–2004)

Acts of Literature, ed. Derek Attridge. London, 1992.
Between the Blinds: A Derrida Reader, ed. Peggy Kamuf. New York, 1991.
Dissemination, trans. and intro. Barbara Johnson. Chicago, 1981.
Of Grammatology, trans. and intro. Gayatri Chakravorty Spivak. Baltimore, MD, 1976.
Writing and Difference, trans. and intro. Alan Bass. London, 1978.

Gérard Genette (1930–)

The Architext: an Introduction, trans. Jane E. Lewin. Berkeley, CA, 1992.
Mimologics, trans. Thaïs E. Morgan, foreword Gerald Prince. Lincoln, NE, 1995.
Narrative Discourse: An Essay on Method, trans. Jane E. Lewin, foreword Jonathan Culler. Ithaca, NY, 1980.
Palimpsests: Literature in the Second Degree, trans. Channa Newman and Claude Doubinsky, foreword Gerald Prince. Lincoln, NE, 1997.

Paratexts: Thresholds of Interpretation, trans. Jane E. Lewin, foreword Richard Macksey. Cambridge, 1997.

Félix Guattari (1930–1992)

(with Gilles Deleuze). *Anti-Oedipus: Capitalism and Schizophrenia*, trans. Robert Hurley, Mark Seem and Helen R. Lane. Minneapolis, MN, 1983.
Chaosmosis: An Ethico-Aesthetic Paradigm, trans. Paul Bains and Julian Pefanis. Sydney, 1995.
The Guattari Reader, ed. Gary Genosko. Oxford, 1996.
Molecular Revolution: Psychiatry and Politics, trans. Rosemary Sheed, intro. David Cooper. Harmondsworth, 1984.
(with Gilles Deleuze). *A Thousand Plateaus: Capitalism and Schizophrenia*, trans. Brian Massumi. Minneapolis, MN, 1987.

Luce Irigaray (1930–)

An Ethics of Sexual Difference, trans. Carolyn Burke and Gillian C. Gill. Ithaca, NY, 1993.
I Love to You: Sketch of a Possible Felicity in History, Ttrans. Alison Martin. New York, 1996.
The Irigaray Reader, ed. Margaret Whitford. Oxford, 1991.
Speculum of the Other Woman, trans. Gillian C. Gill. Ithaca, NY, 1974.
This Sex Which is Not One. Trans. Catherine C. Porter. Ithaca, NY, 1985.

Louis Marin (1931–1992)

To Destroy Painting, trans. Mette Hjort. Chicago, 1995.
Food for Thought, trans. Mette Hjort. Baltimore, MD, 1989.
Portrait of the King, trans. Martha M. Houle. Minneapolis, MN, 1988.
Sublime Poussin, trans. Catherine Porter. Stanford, CA, 1999.
Utopics: The Semiological Play of Textual Spaces, trans. Robert A. Vollrath. Highland Park, NJ, 1984.

Christian Metz (1931–1993)

Film Language: A Semiotics of the Cinema, trans. Michael Taylor. Chicago, IL, 1990.
The Imaginary Signifier: Psychoanalysis and the Cinema, trans. Michael Taylor. Bloomington, IN, 1986.

Guy Debord (1931–1994)

Comments on The Society of the Spectacle, trans. Malcolm Imrie. London, 1998.
Panegyric, trans. James Brook. London, 1991.
The Society of the Spectacle, trans. Donald Nicholson-Smith. Cambridge, MA, 1995.

Umberto Eco (1932–)

Interpretation and Overinterpretation, ed. Stefan Collini. Cambridge, 1992.
The Limits of Interpretation. Bloomington, IN, 1994.
The Role of the Reader: Explorations in the Semiotics of Texts. Bloomington, IN, 1979.
The Search for the Perfect Language, trans. James Fentress. Oxford, 1995.
The Sign of Three: Dupin, Holmes, Peirce, trans. Thomas A. Sebeok. Bloomington, IN, 1988.

Stuart Hall (1932–)

Culture, Media, Language. London, 1990.
Deviancy, Politics and the Media. Birmingham, 1971.
The Hard Road to Renewal: Thatcherism and the Crisis of the Left. London, 1988.

Paul Virilio (1932–)

The Aesthetics of Disappearance, trans. Philip Beitchman. New York, 1991.
The Art of the Motor, trans. Julie Rose. Minneapolis, MN, 1995.
Bunker Archeology, trans. George Collins. New York, 1994.
Open Sky, trans. Julie Rose. London, 1997.
The Vision Machine, trans. Julie Rose. Bloomington, IN, 1994.
War and Cinema: The Logistics of Perception, trans. Patrick Camiller. London, 1989.

Christopher Ricks (1933–)

The Force of Poetry. Oxford, 1995.
Milton's Grand Style. Oxford, 1978.
T. S. Eliot and Prejudice. London, 1994.

Susan Sontag (1933-2004)

Illness as Metaphor and Aids and its Metaphors. London, 2002.
On Photography. London, 1979.
Regarding the Pain of Others. London, 2003.

Fredric Jameson (1934–)

The Ideologies of Theory. 2 vols. Minneapolis, MN, 1988.
The Political Unconscious: Narrative as a Social Symbolic Act. Ithaca, NY, 1981.
Postmodernism or, the Cultural Logic of Late Capitalism. London, 1991.
The Prison-House of Language: A Critical Account of Structuralism and Russian Formalism. Princeton, NJ, 1974.
Signatures of the Visible. New York, 1990.

Sarah Kofman (1934–1994)

Camera Obscura: Of Ideology, trans. Will Straw. London, 1998.
The Enigma of Woman, trans. Catherine Porter. Ithaca, NY, 1985.
Freud and Fiction, trans. Sarah Wykes. Oxford, 1991.
Nietzsche and Metaphor, trans. Duncan Large. London, 1993.
Smothered Words, trans. Madeleine Dobie. Evanston, IL, 1998.

Kate Millett (1934–)

The Politics of Cruelty: An Essay on the Literature of Political Imprisonment. New York, 1990.
Sexual Politics. London, 1977.

Antonio Negri (1934–)

(with Michael Hardt) *Empire.* Cambridge, MA, 2001.
(with Michael Hardt) *Multitude: War and Democracy in the Age of Empire.* London, 2005.
The Savage Anomaly: The Power of Spinoza's Metaphysics and Politics, trans. Michael Hardt. Minneapolis, MN, 1991.

David Lodge (1935–)

The Art of Fiction. London, 1992.
The Language of Fiction: Essays in Criticism and Verbal Analysis of the English Novel. London, 1966.

The Modes of Modern Writing. London, 1977.
The Practice of Writing. London, 1997.

Edward W. Said (1935–2003)

Beginnings. New York, 1985.
Culture and Imperialism. London, 1993.
Orientalism. London, 1978.
Representations of the Intellectual. London, 1994.
The World, the Text, and Critic. Cambridge, MA, 1983.

Benedict Anderson (1936–)

Imagined Communities: Reflections on the Origin and Spread of Nationalism. London, 1983.
Spectres of Comparison: Politics, Culture, and the Nation. London, 1998.
Under Three Flags: Anarchism and the Anti-Colonial Imagination. London, 2005.

Sandra M. Gilbert (1936–)

(with Susan Gubar). *The Mad Woman in the Attic: The Woman Writer and the Nineteenth-Century Literary Imagination.* New Haven, CT, 1988.
(with Susan Gubar). *No Man's Land: The Place of the Woman Writer in the Twentieth Century: Letters from the Front vol. 3.* New Haven, CT, 1994.
(with Susan Gubar). *No Man's Land: The Place of the Woman Writer in the Twentieth Century: Sexchanges vol. 2.* New Haven, CT, 1991.
(with Susan Gubar). *No Man's Land: The Place of the Woman Writer in the Twentieth Century: The War of the Words vol. 1.* New Haven, CT, 1989.
Shakespeare's Sisters. Bloomington, IN, 1981.

Gianni Vattimo (1936–)

The Adventure of Difference: Philosophy after Nietzsche and Heidegger, trans. Cyprian Blamires with Thomas Harrison. Cambridge, 1993.
Belief, trans. Luca D'Isanto and David Webb. Cambridge, 1999.
Beyond Interpretation: The Meaning of Hermeneutics for Philosophy, trans. David Webb. Cambridge, 1997.

The End of Modernity: Nihilism and Hermeneutics in Post-Modern Culture, trans. Jon R. Snyder. Cambridge, 1988.
The Transparent Society trans. David Webb. Cambridge, 1992.

Alain Badiou (1937-)

Ethics: An Essay on the Understanding of Evil, trans. and int. Peter Hallward. London, 2002.
Manifesto for Philosophy, trans., ed., and int. Norman Madarasz. Albany, NY, 1999.
Theoretical Writings, trans. and ed. Ray Brassier and Alberto Toscano. London, 2004.

Hélène Cixous (1938-)

The Exile of James Joyce, trans. Sally A. J. Purcell. New York, 1976.
The Hélène Cixous Reader, ed. Susan Sellers, preface Hélène Cixous, foreword Jacques Derrida. London, 1994.
(with Catherine Clément). *The Newly Born Woman*, trans. Betsy Wing, intro. Sandra Gilbert. Minneapolis, MN, 1975.
Readings: The Poetics of Blanchot, Joyce, Kafka, Lispector, Tsvetaeva, ed. and trans. Verena Conley. London, 1992.
Three Steps on the Ladder of Writing, trans. Sarah Cornell and Susan Sellers. New York, 1993.

Stanley Fish (1938-)

Is There A Text in This Class? The Authority of Interpretive Communities. Cambridge, MA, 1980.
Professional Correctness: Literary Studies and Political Change. Oxford, 1995.
Self-Consuming Artifacts: the Experience of Seventeenth-Century Literature. Berkeley, CA, 1972.
The Stanley Fish Reader. Ed. H. Aram Veeser. Oxford, 1998.
Surprised by Sin: the Reader in 'Paradise Lost'. London, 1967.

Pierre Macherey (1938-)

In a Materialist Way: Selected Essays, ed. Warren Montag, trans. Ted Stolze. London, 1998.
The Object of Literature, trans. David Macey. Cambridge, 1995.
A Theory of Literary Production, trans. Geoffrey Wall. London, 1978.

Carlo Ginzburg (1939–)

The Cheese and the Worms: The Cosmos of a Sixteenth-Century Miller.
Baltimore, MD, 1980.
The Night Battles: Witchcraft and Agrarian Cults in the Sixteenth and Seventeenth Centuries. Baltimore, MD, 1983.
No Island is an Island: Four Glances at English Literature in a World Perspective. New York, 2000.

Germaine Greer (1939–)

The Female Eunuch. London, 1995.
The Madwoman's Underclothes: Essays and Occasional Writings. London, 1987.
Sex and Destiny: The Politics of Human Fertility. Basingstoke, 1985.

Tzvetan Todorov (1939–)

The Conquest of America: The Question of the Other, foreword Anthony Pagden. Trans. Richard Howard. Norman, OK, 1999.
The Fantastic: A Structural Approach to a Literary Genre, trans. Richard Howard, intro. Robert Scholes. Ithaca, NY, 1975.
Genres of Discourse, trans. Catherine Porter. Cambridge, 1990.
Mikhail Bakhtin: The Dialogical Principle, trans. Wlad Godzich. Minneapolis, MN, 1984.
Theories of the Symbol. Trans. Catherine Porter. Ithaca, NY, 1984.

Perry Anderson (1940–)

In the Tracks of Historical Materialism. London, 1983.
Figures in the Forest. London, 2004.
The Origins of Postmodernity. London, 1998.

Philippe Lacoue-Labarthe (1940–)

Heidegger, Art and Politics: The Fiction of the Political, trans. Chris Turner. Oxford, 1990.
Musica Ficta (Figures of Wagner), trans. Felicia McCarren. Stanford, CA, 1994.
Poetry as Experience, trans. Andrea Tarnowski. Stanford, CA, 1999.
(with Jean-Luc Nancy). *The Title of the Letter: A Reading of Lacan*, trans. François Raffoul and David Pettigrew. Albany, NY, 1992.

Typography: Mimesis, Philosophy, Politics, intro. Jacques Derrida. Ed. Christopher Fynsk. Cambridge, MA, 1989.

Jean-Luc Nancy (1940–)

The Birth to Presence, trans. Brian Holmes et al. Stanford, CA, 1993.
The Experience of Freedom, trans. Bridget McDonald, foreword Peter Fenves. Stanford, CA, 1993.
The Inoperative Community, ed. Peter Connor, foreword Christopher Fynsk, trans. Peter Connor et al. Minneapolis, MN, 1991.
The Muses, trans. Peggy Kamuf. Stanford, CA, 1996.
The Sense of the World, trans. and foreword Jeffrey S. Librett. Minneapolis, MN, 1997.

Julia Kristeva (1941–)

Desire in Language: A Semiotic Approach to Literature and Art, ed. Leon S. Roudiez, trans. Thomas Gora et al. New York, 1980.
The Kristeva Reader, ed. Toril Moi. Oxford, 1986.
Powers of Horror: An Essay on Abjection, trans. Leon S. Roudiez. New York, 1982.
Revolution in Poetic Language, trans. Margaret Waller, intro. Leon S. Roudiez. New York, 1984.
Tales of Love, trans. Leon S. Roudiez. New York, 1987.

Elaine Showalter (1941–)

The Female Malady: Women, Madness, and English Culture, 1830–1980. London, 1987.
Hystories: Hysterical Epidemics and Modern Culture. London, 1998.
A Literature of their Own: British Women Novelists from Brontë to Lessing. London, 1978.
Sexual Anarchy: Gender and Culture at the Fin de Siècle. London, 1992.
Sister's Choice: Tradition and Change in American Women's Writing. Oxford, 1995.

Giorgio Agamben (1942–)

Language and Death: The Place of Negativity, trans. Karen E. Pinkus with Michael Hardt. Minneapolis, MN, 1991.
Stanzas: Word and Phantasm in Western Culture, trans. Ronald L. Martinez. Minneapolis, MN, 1993.

Idea of Prose, trans. Michael Sullivan and Sam Whitsitt. Albany, NY, 1995.
Homo Sacer: Sovereign Power and Bare Life. Trans. Daniel Heller-Roazen. Stanford, CA, 1998.
The End of the Poem: Studies in Poetics, trans. Daniel Heller-Roazen. Stanford, CA, 1999.

Gayatri Chakravorty Spivak (1942–)

A Critique of Postcolonial Reason: Toward a History of the Vanishing Present. Cambridge, MA, 1999.
In Other Worlds: Essays in Cultural Politics. London, 1987.
Outside in the Teaching Machine. London, 1993.
The Spivak Reader, eds. Donna Landry and Gerald MacLean. London, 1996.
Thinking Academic Freedom in Gendered Postcoloniality. Cape Town, 1992.

Etienne Balibar (1942–)

The Philosophy of Marx, trans. Chris Turner. London, 1995.
Politics and the Other Scene, trans. Daniel Hahn. London, 1999.
(with Immanuel Wallerstein). *Race, Nation, Class: Ambiguous Identities*, trans. Chris Turner. London, 1991.
Spinoza and Politics, trans. Peter Snowdon. London, 1998.

Terry Eagleton (1943–)

Criticism and Ideology: A Study in Marxist Literary Theory. London, 1975.
The Function of Criticism: From the Spectator to Post-Structuralism. London, 1984.
The Ideology of the Aesthetic. Oxford, 1990.
Ideology: an Introduction. London, 1991.
The Illusions of Postmodernism. Oxford, 1996.

Stephen Greenblatt (1943–)

Learning to Curse: Essays in Early Modern Culture. New York, 1990.
Marvellous Possessions: The Wonder of the New World. Chicago, 1991.
Renaissance Self-Fashioning from More to Shakespeare. Chicago, 1980.
Shakespearean Negotiations: The Circulation of Social Energy in Renaissance England. Berkeley, CA, 1988.

Sir Walter Ralegh: The Renaissance Man and His Roles. New Haven, CT, 1973.

Susan Gubar (1944–)

Critical Condition: Feminism at the Turn of the Century. New York, 2000.
Racechanges: White Skin, Black Face in American Culture. Oxford, 1997.

Donna Haraway (1944–)

The Haraway Reader. London, 1997.
Modest Witness: Feminism and Technoscience. London, 1997.
Simians, Cyborgs, and Women: The Reinvention of Nature. London, 1991.

Catherine Gallagher (1945–)

The Industrial Reformation of English Fiction: Social Discourse and Narrative Form 1832–1867. Chicago, 1985.
Nobody's Story: the Vanishing Acts of Women Writers in the Marketplace, 1670–1820. Berkeley, 1995.
(with Stephen Greenblatt). *Practicing the New Historicism.* Chicago, 2000.

Andrea Dworkin (1946–2005)

Pornography: Men Possessing Women. London, 1981.
Women Hating: A Radical Look at Sexuality. London, 1976.

Peggy Kamuf (1947–)

The Division I of Literature or the University in Deconstruction. Chicago, 1997.
Signature Pieces: On the Institution of Authorship. Ithaca, NY, 1988.
Book of Addresses. Stanford, CA, 2005.

Camille Paglia (1947–)

Break, Blow, Burn: Camille Paglia reads Forty-Three of the World's Best Poems. New York, 2005.
Sex, Art, and American Culture: Essays. London, 1993.

Sexual Personae: Art and Decadence from Nefertiti to Emily Dickinson. New York, 1991.

Homi K. Bhabha (1949–)

The Location of Culture. London, 1994.

Slavoj Žižek (1949–)

Enjoy Your Symptom! London, 1992.
For They Know Not What They Do: Enjoyment as a Political Factor. London, 1991.
The Plague of Fantasies. London, 1997.
The Sublime Object of Ideology. London, 1989.
Tarrying With the Negative. Durham, NC, 1993.

Henry Louis Gates, Jr (1950–)

Figures in Black: Words, Signs, and the Racial Self. Oxford, 1987.
The Signifying Monkey: Towards a Theory of Afro-American Literary Criticism. Oxford, 1990.
Thirteen Ways of Looking at a Black Man. New York, 1998

Eve Kosofsky Sedgwick (1950–)

Between Men: English Literature and Male Homosocial Desire. New York, 1985.
A Dialogue on Love. Boston, 2000.
Epistemology of the Closet. Berkeley, CA, 1990.
Fat Art, Thin Art. Durham, NC, 1994.
Tendencies. London, 1994.

bell hooks (1952–)

Ain't I a Woman? Black Women and Feminism. London, 1983.
Outlaw Culture: Resisting Representation. London, 1994.
Reel to Real: Race, Sex, and Class at the Movies. London, 1997.

Toril Moi (1953–)

Simone de Beauvoir: The Making of an Intellectual Woman. Oxford, 1994.
What is a Woman? And other Essays. Oxford, 2000.

Judith Butler (1956–)

Bodies that Matter: On the Discursive Limits of 'Sex'. New York, 1993.
Excitable Speech: A Politics of the Performative. London, 1997.
Gender Trouble: Feminism and the Subversion of Identity, new edn. London, 1999.
The Psychic Life of Power: Theories in Subjection. Stanford, CA, 1997.
Subjects of Desire: Hegelian Reflections in Twentieth-Century France, new edn. New York, 1999.

Avital Ronell (1956–)

Finitude's Score: Essays for the End of the Millenium. Lincoln, NE, 1994.
Literature, Addiction, Mania. Lincoln, NE, 1992.
Stupidity. Urbana, IL, 2001.
The Telephone Book: Technology, Schizophrenia, Electric Speech. Lincoln, NE, 1989.